ABOUT THE AUTHOR

Positive. Inspiring. Empowering. Mike is a humble leader who believes in doing everything to the best of his abilities, especially motivating others to be their best! A teacher and coach for 25 years, Mike has received numerous accolades at multiple levels for his positive and infectious teaching and coaching. Mike is known as a Champion for students, teachers and coaches. Mike is also a powerful speaker for schools, teachers, coaches and leaders.

Contact him for speaking via his website at mike-franklin.com

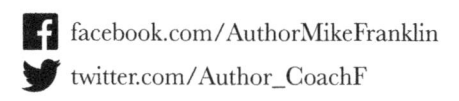

facebook.com/AuthorMikeFranklin
twitter.com/Author_CoachF

TEACHER FUEL

MIKE FRANKLIN

This book is dedicated to all of the teachers fighting the good fight and the amazing family members who support them. Thank You Kristie, Kaylee, Haylee and Kathan.

CONTENTS

Foreword   ix

1. Mouth-to-Ear Resuscitation   1
2. Not All Heroes Wear Capes   17
3. Mission Critical   31
4. The Lies   45
5. A Checkup from the Neck Up   61
6. Take Over the Makeover   75
7. Modus Operandi   91
8. Rent's Due   105
9. High-Performance Learning   119
10. A Healthy You   135
11. Run at the Giant   151

Get in touch   163

FOREWORD

In recent years the demands of teaching have exceeded anything we could have been prepared for. There have been extraordinary challenges. Educators have had to completely revamp everything they knew about instruction, assessing and building relationships. We hit a sink or swim moment. Our students needed us regardless of the fatigue, pressures, or tolls that it would take on educators. Even fine-tuned machines break down when they are pushed to the brink of exhaustion. I worry about the toll that the last few years has taken on teachers and administrators. I have visited many school systems and routinely hear the same thing. People in our profession are exhausted and morale is at an all time low.

My hope and intent for this book is to bring passion back to careers. I want to remind educators of the fire that they have burning deep inside. I want to focus on the positive things that made each of you special and invaluable beyond measure. I want this book to remind you and your staff the amazing difference that you make and the dreams that you build for a lifetime. May this book bring the energy, passion, and enthusiasm inside you back to life and result in changing lives. Thank you for serving kids.

1
MOUTH-TO-EAR RESUSCITATION

"Happiness is a choice that requires effort at times."

— Aeschylus

You didn't get into the profession of teaching, coaching, tutoring, band directing, or any other school-based job for the money. If you did, we gotta find another book for you, like *How to Fix a Very Bad Plan*.

I'm mostly kidding, but in reality, you are in teaching because of your ideologies. You believe in the good that exists in our young people. You believe in serving our students academically and socially, and also with their mental health and development. You got into this profession because you believe you can be used as a tool—and there is no better tool in all of education for kids than a teacher who is on fire!

So maybe over the last many years, you have dedicated your life to serving our young people. You have been an uplifter, a good finder, and a motivator as often as possible. You have shown up early and stayed late for the sake of putting in your best effort for your students. You've taken on various school responsibilities on top of teaching to give even more of yourself. I'm going to pause right here and say... "THANK YOU." Thank you so much for the sacrifices that you have made for kids.

But perhaps somewhere along the way, that pace became tougher and tougher to sustain. The emerging negativity, politics, and problems in education have worn you down. Simply put, you're tired. Let's face it, this is a profession where it's very easy to get burned out. You are not the first great teacher that this has happened to and you won't be the last. You're in a rut and you've lost that pep in your step. It's okay not to be okay, you've earned that. Now... it's time to take your passion back!

Lies, distractions, problems, and mindsets can make you forget who you are and what made you great. It's time to go back to the you that you used to be. It's time to face the lies, the distractions, and the problems. Most of all, it's time to take control of your mind again.

Perspective

I think a great place to start is perspective. Often the very problems that we are complaining about, others are praying for. What if all we had today was what we said we were thankful for out loud yesterday? How much would we have? We get angry because our computer might take ten seconds instead of five to get us the answer to a question that we Googled. Have we forgotten how it used to work not all that long ago? Two words: card catalog. We used to have to go into the library and search for the location of a book to actually read through, which *might* have had the answer in it. And that is assuming that nobody removed the card from its place in the catalog. I was so bad at that, it might have taken me three hours to get that one answer. Perspective is a powerful tool.

A British shoe company sent two representatives to a jungle village to test the potential for shoe sales. The first employee reported, "There is absolutely no potential for sales here, nobody wears shoes." The second employee reported, "There is an incredible potential for sales here, nobody wears shoes." Which employee are we?

Getting your passion and happiness back begins with you making a conscious decision to change your current perspective. There is a lot wrong with the way the education system works now, and it is really easy to let it get the best of you some days. We have all been there. Put a few of those days together and it can change you if you let it. Giving each negative interaction its own perspective can help.

A popular example is worrying about what others think. In any given situation, you can rarely make everybody happy. You are going to have tough decisions and tough fights on your hands sometimes because that's just the nature of leadership. Students, parents, administrators, and even board members may not like you. Do what you know to be right and that's a perspective you will live well with. Sir Winston Churchill brilliantly said, "You have enemies? Good. That means you've stood up for something, sometime in your life." Instead of giving the negativity your energy, simply change your perspective. Great leaders like Churchill had to.

When you think about your future in education, I want you to use perspective. What were your passions once and what did you love about this job? A mentor and close friend of mine moved from a teaching to a school support position. He was great at teaching and really cared about students. When he moved to the school support position, he shined even more than he did as a teacher. He could take a student who was having their worst day and in minutes have them laughing and ready to return to class.

He later decided to become an assistant principal. He was very good at that as well, but I felt like he wasn't able to see students or use the gifts that he had with students as much. I could tell that was weighing on him. Eventually, he courageously moved back down the pay scale to do what he loved, returning to school support. He had such a great perspective. A courageous battle with lymphoma couldn't deter him either. He used that experience for fuel and perspective with each and every relationship he had in our building and became a true game-changer for students and teachers alike.

The Old Man on the Beach

When I am being selfish and feel sorry for myself because I have some issue, I love being reminded to have perspective through stories like this one. A young business executive was having a stressful day and couldn't handle the chaos in his office a minute longer. Stressed and angry he stormed out of the building and walked down to the beach. There he saw a poor old man dressed in ragged clothes relaxing on a beach chair with a fishing rod nearby.

Without a care in the world, the old man didn't seem to notice or care that his rod was bent. The businessman said, "Hey, you have a fish on your line mister. You better hurry up and reel him in." The old man looked almost annoyed as he rose out of his chair to reel the fish in. "Wow, that is a big one!" the young man said. You could see the wheels turning in the young man's head as he spoke again and said, "You should sell that fish to the market."

With a grin the old man said, "Then what?" Perplexed by the question, the young executive responded, "Well, then you buy another rod and catch twice as many fish and make double the money." The old man responded, "Then what?" The young man paused for a second before saying, "You can use that money to buy a boat and some nets. Now the fish and the money would be rolling in."

Again the old man responded, "Then what?" Annoyed, the young man replied, "Simple, you use that money to buy a whole fleet of boats, hire more fishermen and maybe a processing center so you can sell the fish yourself to cut costs." Yet again the old man responded, "Then what?" The young man was really perplexed. He paused and said, "Well, after doing that for a few years you could retire and just happily relax on a beach somewhere for all of your remaining days." The poor old man looked at the businessman and said with a smirk, "What do you think I was doing before you showed up?"

That is a great perspective. Whether it's teaching or how we navigate our personal lives, we should be questioning motives and questioning the process before we jump in. It could save you tons of time and energy.

Appreciation

Another tool for regaining your passion is the use of appreciation. In this busy life it is so very easy to take beautiful things and beautiful people for granted. Sometimes we need to take a deep breath and look at life through a different lens.

When I try to motivate kids, I like to use appreciation as their motivation. Start with how they view school. In 2020 the average cost to educate a student in the United States was $12,612 per student per year. From Kindergarten to graduation, that's thirteen years of school for a total cost of $163,956 per student. If you stack that money in front of a student, I doubt they would turn it away.

But sadly, some students *will* turn it away. We have to make students understand that their education is their $163,956 gift. That's their money. That money can be used to make a good life for themselves after school if used right. Maybe changing to that perspective and understanding will get some students to change the value they put in school.

I'm sure that you have heard of the term "one-track mind" before. A pessimist's mind has been trained to see the doom in everything. An optimist's mind has been trained to see the good in everything. A go-getter's mind is wired to see the opportunity in everything. And a problem-solver's mind is wired to see the solution in everything. When we focus on one thing, we usually become pretty good over time at that one thing.

Try going one day focusing on appreciating everything that your eyes see. Have you ever heard of the game Six Degrees of Separation? It's a game where players compete to take almost any Hollywood actor and link them by way of establishing a path of films and stars to famed actor Kevin Bacon—any actor is said to be no more than six links away from him.

Well, what if you did that with appreciation? What if you made a sincere effort to relate everything and everyone you cross paths with on a given day to something you appreciate? I have to believe that that kind of appreciation would change you. And I'm not talking just about the good events that happened or the people you have a fondness for. That's easy. I'm talking about the little parts of the job that you've grown to dislike and people that you don't have a strong affinity for.

You may not like or appreciate a job but there's something in it that probably could be flipped for your growth and development if you viewed it right. I can complain that a school employee didn't clean my classroom to my satisfaction, or I can take pride in cleaning my own room and freeing up time for that employee to work hard elsewhere. I can turn a negative feeling into one of accomplishment and show appreciation in my school and my room. I can even involve students in the work and get them to grow an appreciation for our classroom and its aesthetics. It beats complaining, doesn't it?

You might not enjoy some of your duties. Maybe instead of viewing lunch duty as a waste of your time, you appreciate this task as an opportunity to grow relationships with students at lunch. Work the room and let the students who you don't see in your classroom know you and your awesomeness.

You may not appreciate every colleague that you work with either. But you can appreciate something that they do if you look hard enough. Accountability, structure, discipline, or even punctuality are things we can appreciate instead of being negative and focusing on what we don't like about them.

Focusing on appreciation doesn't just start and stop in the workplace. Appreciate your commute to work by valuing what you can accomplish during that time. You can listen to some type of calming music to meditate and get your mind into a high-performing state. You can play a TED Talk on some area of your focused growth. You can rehearse a speech, strategize a meeting or intervention, or even work on your teacher tone. The possibilities are endless. Or you could choose to believe you have the worst job and the worst luck, and that everybody else is to blame for your unhappiness.

Covid was terrible but it made me appreciate many things. Being trapped in my house really made me appreciate simple walks, views of mountains, and colors of the seasons. Most of all, it made me appreciate time. I am so thankful for the blessing of time that I was given to spend with my family. Typically, I overschedule and then stress about the next place I have to be. Instead of looking at all of the things I couldn't do or places that I couldn't go, I enjoyed thinking about the blessings that I had in front of me.

If you are showing up to work and not loving what you do, then start doing what you love. Are you teaching from the heart? Teaching is an art, and not everyone can do it. And what I know about art is that it is all about expressing your creativity. There is no law that says you can't be creative in teaching and make it fun.

When it feels like work, it is. Steve Jobs said, "Your work is going to fill a large part of your life, and the only way to be truly satisfied is to do what you believe is great work. And the only way to do great work is to love what you do." If I am going to do something for eight to twelve hours a day, I'm going to find the joy in it. I'm going to have some fun with it.

Ways to Make Your Workday Fun

- Start your day with a mood-setter before you enter the building. A workout, a good coffee, a fun snack, or a faith-based reading will prepare your mood for the day ahead.
- Add happy music to your day. Play it while planning or use it in a lesson with your classes. Something that gets your foot tapping can't be bad for your attitude.
- Take movement-based brain breaks with your class. Have fun with it. Maybe Simon Says or a mock roller-coaster ride will get them and you smiling.
- Give yourself something to look forward to at lunch. It's halftime! Use food or exercise to make you happy.
- Involve others. Class competitions or teacher-to-teacher challenges can be a source of motivation and enjoyment.

Use Fun to Regain Passion

If you want to start your day on the right foot, do something for yourself before you enter the building. For me, a good, strong coffee always puts me in a great mood and makes the car ride enjoyable. For others, maybe a sweet treat is the ticket. Pay it forward and bring an extra one for a coworker to set their mood too. Maybe on a Friday, get crazy and bring the whole department a dozen doughnuts or bagels and have the happiest group in the school.

You can find the right frame of mind and even get into shape with a before-school walk, run, or strength-training session in your school's gymnasium or weight room. Chances are there won't be a crowd at that time. Looking for a mental workout instead? Be stubborn about your time and set aside thirty minutes in solitude to read something that grows your faith or intellect. It's like putting your armor on for the day's battles ahead.

Every teacher should have something positive built into their lunchtime to feel good about. Think of lunch as a teacher's halftime. The day is 50 percent over and you have time to reset yourself for the second half. What can you do in thirty minutes? For some, it's nutrition and a well-deserved mental timeout while enjoying the camaraderie of your colleagues. I'm pretty weird and I don't eat during the day so I like to spend my thirty minutes lifting weights or walking bleacher steps as my halftime routine. Maybe a short meditation session is your thing. The point is, do what makes you happy and prepares you to go into the rest of your day with a smile.

Another way to make your job fun is to add some competitiveness to your day by challenging others to a competition. Maybe you challenge a similar class to an "academic Olympics," comparing class scores or averages. This could add the element of fun and increase engagement. You can challenge another teacher in any area of self-improvement too. Try to see who can read the most books, lose the most weight, or raise the most funds for a worthwhile charity. This can change your view and elevate others' moods as well.

Perhaps the greatest asset to finding your passion again is simply to think positive. I realize that this is a "chicken or the egg" scenario. If you loved your job, you would be thinking positive. But the more that I read, the more that I believe the only way you can be positive is to know that it's a conscious effort and it won't just appear naturally.

Being a Positive Thinker

In 2005, the National Science Foundation published results from a study on the human brain and how it generates thought. It concluded that the average human being has about 12,000 to 60,000 thoughts per day. Of those, 95 percent were repetitions from the day before. And 80 percent of all of them were negative. That tells me two things. First, we have a lot of random thoughts. Second, left alone our brains are mostly wired to be negative.

This means that having a positive mindset takes work. It's a daily decision with action. If I hooked a new battery up to my car and it didn't work, I'd rewire it right away. Our brains need conscious rewiring from time to time. I know that mine does. There are enough negative forces in trying to educate our young people, so I don't need to be another one. My mindset each day is going to be my choice. When I signed that teaching contract, I wasn't promised an easy career or a bad career, I was promised a career. What I do with that career is up to me.

Are you a worrier? That's negative thinking too. Dr. Robert Leahy is a renowned professor of psychology at Weill Cornell Medical College, and he explains that in studies, 85 percent of what patients worried about never happened. And of the 15 percent who did experience their fear happening, approximately eight out of ten discovered that they handled it better than they expected.

High anxiety levels trigger hormones that make our hearts beat faster and harder, which can lead to high blood pressure, heart attacks, and strokes. The fact is, these potential fears are never going to stop coming at us, so we might as well change our views to change our health. A worry-free you and a positive you will be a better teacher for our young people.

Happiness in teaching can be as easy as redefining our job description. A job *description* doesn't have to be a job *restriction*. The description is going to tell me what I have to do but...it's not going to tell me what I can't do. After I check all the boxes related to educating students, I am allowed to do more. There is an expression in teaching that we are in the business of selling funeral tickets. Our tickets. Meaning, relationships are critical for a meaningful career.

Having positive relationships with the people you are spending seven to ten hours a day with sure sounds like it would make me more passionate about my job. I can't imagine a job where you are staring at the clock all day without the engagement of your students. Those relationships are not just for them, they are medicine for us too. For me, I feed off their happiness. They keep me feeling young, energetic, and alive. Tapping into your students' happiness and energy is like finding the fountain of youth. I love celebrating their successes with them.

If you asked me to pick just one way to love your job, no matter how much garbage you might be dealing with, I would say to you: Find their joy and you'll find your joy. Everything could be going wrong around me—school finances, tough relations with leaders, etc., but watching one of my students smile and feel happy sends pleasure to my brain. If they smile, I smile. There is no complicated methodology. Start making your class fun again. Start building in fun moments and celebrate their successes and smiles with them. Sure, negativity is contagious but so is happiness, and doggone it...I'm just not missing out on that.

Their JOY, Your JOY Moments

- Ask a student to tell you the greatest moment of their life...it will be like you were there for it.
- Ask a student what a perfect day looks like to them...you'll picture it too.
- Ask a student to make a face that an emoji couldn't capture. No way you don't laugh!
- Ask a student what they are most proud of...you'll be proud.
- Ask a student what brings them joy in school...maybe you'll realize it brings you joy too.

The average lifespan is about seventy-two years or roughly 26,280 days. Think about how real that would look to you if you had those days marked on a wall and had to erase one each night before you went to bed. If you change your mindset, would that change your habits? Would the things that you stress about as a teacher, coach, or leader be different or less important?

So before you spend another one of your valuable 26,280 days being unhappy, ask yourself one question: "When I erased a day before falling asleep, did I erase a mark that represented growth, enhanced relationships, or served someone? Or was it just another mark on the wall with nothing to be happy about?" Make each mark mean something.

Nightly "Not Missing the Mark" Marks

- I did something new that I haven't done before.
- I went somewhere that I have never been before.
- I was an uplifter. I sent a positive email, letter, or text to someone.
- I served one person today who needed serving.
- I addressed one bad habit that I have.
- I created a new or stronger relationship with one person.
- I did one thing for my mental health and one for my physical health.
- I became wiser today with something I targeted as essential for me to research.

The average American spends five hours a day on their phone and checks it an average of fifty-eight times. That's the equivalent of thirty-five hours a week. So if life is time management, what are your time distractions?

Your Attitude Is Your Superpower

Can you envision yourself being so committed to doing something great that you want to take away anything that could stop you? I am talking about a level where giving 99 percent is a failure. A new and better version of you as a teacher and as a leader is as simple as flipping a switch in your mind that says, "I am becoming a new person this minute and I am never looking back." That person is in you, right here and right now.

Historical figures have taught me that my methodology matters when I commit to doing something spectacular and grand. If we want something bad enough, we have to be willing to take mighty risks to gain mighty rewards. Your mindset has to be that no one else is concerned about your success, so you must be the one to control your destiny. Such was the case for Captain Cortez when he sailed to Mexico to battle for the Aztec Empire. Upon arrival, Cortez ordered that every boat be set on fire. That left both he and his men with two simple options; win or be killed. His troops were all in at that point and there was no turning back.

The term "Point of no return" originated in the aviation sector. It is defined as the point during a flight at which an aircraft is no longer capable of returning to its origin of takeoff due to fuel considerations. Making the bold decision to pass the point of no return is a full commitment and an all-in scenario. If you and I are truly committed to taking it up a level, this applies to us.

In 1919, a cash prize of $25,000 was offered to the first pilot to fly nonstop from New York City to Paris. This motivated a few pilots, four of which were killed in their attempts while others simply turned around in flight. For Charles Lindbergh the real motivation was doing something grand that had never been done before.

Lindbergh was both focused and committed. Every other pilot that attempted this lofty goal used a multi-engine design. A second engine could be a lifesaver if the other engine failed. Lindbergh was all-in and chose to use a lighter single engine for his attempt. Almost all of the other ventures included co-pilots for their operation. The demands of a flight of this length would push the limits in the areas of navigation, sleep, and mental fortitude. Lindbergh chose to store more fuel over taking the help. He also declined to take a parachute or radio. Metaphorically speaking, Lindbergh burned his ships, with his life at stake.

He was criticized by newspapers who referred to him as, "The flying fool."

On May 20, 1927, at 7:52 a.m., Lindbergh took off from New York. After 33 ½ hours and over 3,600 miles later, Charles Lindbergh did the impossible and successfully landed in Paris.

Here's why that story matters to you and me today. Heroes and historical figures were ordinary people. It was their commitment, process, and passion that allowed them to separate themselves and accomplish mighty things. They are not made special, they are driven. If you want to be the best teacher around, then do it. Make your lofty goal. Burn your ships, pass the point of no return and go for it! The truth is that you were made in the same likeness as these historical figures. There's nothing you can't do so go chase your dreams.

You have been given an amazing superpower to make your "mark" on this world. You were not made from average parts and you weren't made from junk. You were made perfect, for a purpose, and your journey isn't a lonely one. You were made to cross paths with hundreds, if not thousands, of young and impressionable lives. I don't believe in coincidence. I believe that the culmination of all the good days, and certainly the bad days as well, have made you ready for the next student that you are about to see. You are not finished. Until you collect that fruit basket from your colleagues on the last day of your career, you have more to do. If you feel like you are in a motivational rut…. let's change stuff up. Let's change the significance of that mark you erase from the wall tonight!

2

NOT ALL HEROES WEAR CAPES

"A hero is no braver than an ordinary man, but he is brave five minutes longer."

— RALPH WALDO EMERSON

Never underestimate the amazing power that comes with teaching. Think about the best day that you could have in another job. A stockbroker can make a company a million dollars today. An architect can complete a significant building for a city today. And a professional athlete can be inducted into the Hall of Fame today. But in all reality, each of these feats falls short of our best days in working with young people.

In each of those careers, the rewards of those "great" days probably feel really good, and I'd imagine people in those careers get rewarded with a sense of accomplishment and something nice that's extrinsic as well. But those rewards aren't living and they aren't breathing. The stockbroker gets a nice check, but that money likely won't last too long. As educators, we have the power to take something and add everlasting value to it. We can add purpose, direction, and hope to a life. That's right, our trophies and paychecks come in the way of living human beings. To borrow a line from a famous commercial, "We don't make these things...we make these things better."

We can take a young person who is doing all the right things and reassure them with our simple praise. We can build their momentum and reinforce in them that they are destined for greatness. We can take an average-performing student and show them the untapped potential they have deep down inside. With that confidence, they can conquer their insecurities and shortcomings to make their mark on this world. We can take a young person who has no idea how loved or valuable they are and instill hope and purpose in them. This lights my soul! Keep your paychecks, I'll take this every time, all the time. My trophies are walking and breathing, and they have the potential to do anything they want.

Superheroes become super from doing amazing things for the good of other people. Think about that. Superman is super because he cares. He cares enough to get involved and he cares enough to make sure that somebody who isn't okay becomes okay. Then when that situation is safe, he goes out and finds the next person to help. Day after day and year after year. Hmmm, what other job does that?!

Chances are that you can immediately think of a teacher or coach who brought out the best in you. They just understood you, grew you, and cared enough to really get to know you. The relationship and impact they had with you probably has you feeling the "warm fuzzies" right now. That feeling you're having is called gratitude, and it was built with valuable time and love that someone invested in you. When you invest in other people, you build connections and relationships that are stronger than words. They are feelings like the ones you're having now for that person who believed in you many years ago. Time will fade but at the mention of their name, your feelings for what they did for you will not. That, my friends, is the power of the relationships we build.

Winning Traits

Legendary teachers have winning personality traits. I am a big fan of the power of praise, and I talk about that often. Giving praise is easy, but taking it can sometimes be uncomfortable. It's a slippery slope because we were made to be humble and not accept the glory ourselves. The flipside is that we need to be confident in our efforts. Confidence is believing that you can get the job done. Arrogance is believing that your job is more important than anyone else's. Confident teachers believe in executing their school's mission, while arrogant teachers believe in executing their own mission. Humility is a keystone trait and is important in bringing groups together. Be humble or be humbled, because humility is coming. No matter who we are, we're all just one phone call away from our knees. Even Superman had kryptonite.

When you are in the business of serving others (i.e., teaching), your disposition is really important. It's like Goldilocks's taste in porridge, we don't want it too hot or too cold, it has to be just right. If you come in too hot like a dictator, you will lose the ability to relate to students. Your class will have the feel of a sweatshop, as if you are the boss and they are just workers. If you are too humble or too meek, the feel of the class will be a free-for-all. There is no leadership, and chaos ensues. It's such a delicate balance.

So lead humbly but...you need to own a few positive things on the inside. Own that you are amazing! Own that you are a great teacher, a great administrator, or a great coach to young people. I'm dead serious. Own that you care about kids and you care about being better today than you were yesterday. Own that you are not lazy and you work hard to do a great job and truly make a difference.

Own that being a teacher, administrator, or coach means something to you, and when someone asks you what you do for a living, with your shoulders held back you say, "I'm an educator." If that person responds, "I'm an executive who's made millions," just give them that look that implies that your answer buries theirs. Wear who you are like a badge of honor. You gotta believe in what you do. It all starts there.

What You Should Be Saying EVERY SINGLE DAY!

- *I can* flat-out teach. I know I was made for this.
- *I can* see something truly amazing happening to me in this job.
- *I can* be more organized, more student focused, and more productive than I was yesterday.
- *I can* grow my relationships with at least five people I encounter today.
- *I can* do something kind for someone today that will impact them in a positive way.
- *I can* say something to uplift and make someone else better today.

Zig Ziglar says, "You cannot perform in a manner inconsistent with the way you see yourself." That is spot on. I'm going to be completely honest, I really struggle with this sometimes. I do not believe that I was made any better than anyone else, because I wasn't. And I know that talent is given, so I need to always be humble and praise where any gifts came from. So how can I see myself as being great and gifted?

It's simple, we were all made gifted and for a purpose. We don't all have the same gifts or the same purpose. That's why you have to be you. You can't be like that other teacher, even if they are great. You have to find out what strengths you have been given and how you can shine. So own that you were made special. There were no junk materials used when you were made. Own your greatness and see yourself doing great things. If you see average, then that's exactly what you and your students are going to get.

Do you know what your superpower is? I really enjoy meeting great teachers. When you have a few together, it's fun to see how different they all look. Good teaching looks like good teaching, but it doesn't look the exact same from every good teacher. Maybe one teacher is successful because they are cerebral while another is successful because they are not. One teacher is known for their professionalism at all times while another is known for their ability to get down to the level of all students. A grizzly bear has to hunt like a grizzly bear and a chameleon like a chameleon. The chameleon wouldn't do well trying to use the grizzly bear's skillset nor the other way around. As educators, we have to discover the gifts that we have been blessed with and use them to build ourselves into the next great superhero!

Potential Superpowers Educators May Have

- Natural leadership—A Pied Piper
- Energy—ADHD used correctly can be a sincere asset
- Calmness—Your ship can take on water and keep sailing
- Flexibility—Being able to find other ways to get it done
- Relating—An ability to connect with others
- Caring—A desire to help others
- Humor—A power that can break down walls and build relationships
- Love—You can have a long career on this one alone

So what can you and I give? You may think you have little to give as a teacher. You may think you don't possess much creativity. You may think you don't possess much talent. Maybe you believe that you just don't have much to give. I disagree, you have something really special.

Hear me when I say this: You can give others the greatest thing you have. You can give them YOU. You can give students your personal attention. You might be the only one all day that calls a student by their name. You can give students your love and empathy. You might be the only one willing to listen to their story when they need someone to stop the momentum that's spiraling out of control. And you can give kids your reputation. Let them know that day in and day out, you are a person they can trust, one who has no agenda except to help them and care about them.

10 Things in Teaching That Requires Zero Talent

1. Passion
2. A positive attitude
3. Showing up and being present while there
4. Doing something randomly nice for a coworker
5. Doing extra for students
6. Work ethic
7. Welcoming students to your room by their names
8. Contributing to a school's positive culture
9. Knowing more about a student than their grade
10. Giving out praise

Look in the mirror. What do you see? I've never been diagnosed, but I'm 99.9% sure I've had ADHD my whole life. I've always seen that in my mirror. When I started teaching, I hid that from everyone. I pretended to be stoic and professional at all costs, showing no emotion and simply educating. That works for some teachers, but that did not work for me. After a few months of teaching, I noticed a student hiding behind a set of bleachers in the gym during their lunch break. That's when my life as a teacher changed.

I used my professional voice and said, "Excuse me, all students need to be in areas with direct supervision at all times. You need to return to the cafeteria." I was not prepared for the student's reply. As I got closer, I saw "the Look." If you are a teacher, you know what look that I am talking about, the look a student gives you that screams, "I'm in a dark place. I'm scared. I need your help." It's probably something like a mother's intuition—you see it and you just know.

The student's eyes were welling up with tears as she started to rise. That's when I changed everything I knew about teaching. Figuratively speaking, I went into my phone booth and came out with my superhero costume on. My special power….ADHD and an ability to get to a common ground with students. That's it, I'm not gifted. I'm not smart. I'm not much of anything, but I am me and I am willing to offer that to you.

I introduced myself and got to know this student. As you can imagine there were some serious things going on in her family life, things that no young person should have to worry about. It broke my heart. I hadn't had much experience with this, and I didn't have any answers. I just listened and when she was done, that's when my fiery ADHD superpower took over. I was the Hulk and I had just turned green. I found energy and words from somewhere, and I made case after case to this student explaining why she was going to push through this and turn out amazing. Seeing that young person walk away with hope just felt right. I never looked back.

That's just one story, my story. Your story needs to be written with your pen and your superpower. If you have charisma and natural leadership, think of the possibilities. What positive cause could you lead young people to? Could you use your charisma to change the culture in a school? Some of you are Pied Pipers and have the power to make kindness, equity, and treating everybody well the new trend that sweeps your building.

Some of you have been blessed with an amazing sense of humor. You can use that to connect with students. I've never seen people laugh and be in a negative mood at the same time. Laughter is a mood changer. Your humor can turn moods, and turning moods is a serious superpower needed in classrooms.

Mother Teresa said, "It is easier to give a cup of rice to relieve hunger than to relieve the loneliness and pain of someone unloved." Your superpower might be love, kindness, or a spirit of giving. Our world needs you! You people are game-changers. You change students with your empathy to hear them when they hurt. You change schools with random and thoughtful "pay it forward" acts of kindness. You change communities with your dedication to solvable problems like hunger, or by lending a helping hand when someone needs it most. Your talents are more crucial than ever.

Momentum

I enjoy the lessons that different teaching and coaching experiences have taught me. It's amazing how often they cross over and help me. For example, in coaching, sometimes a team gets on a roll. The environment has suddenly and completely changed. Momentum in one direction has stopped and is clearly building in another direction. It often impacts the performance of the fans and the athletes.

If your team does something well, the crowd erupts and empowers you. All of a sudden, your team is able to perform at a higher level. The impact of the environment has your players performing out of their minds. It's like they are on autopilot but at their highest levels.

I came to understand that teaching can work the same way. When I see a student doing something right, I can be like the people in that crowd. I can cheer them on with praise, creating that same outstanding momentum that pushes them higher. As you cheer on your students, you are changing the environment. You build curiosity in them about how far they can ride this well-performing wave. You can empower them to keep climbing to new heights.

Sometimes as a coach you are on the other side of that experience. In an instant and without notice, the momentum can turn the other way. Suddenly, it is all going the wrong way for your team. The environment has turned against you, and your team can't do a thing right. The crowd is against you, and one mistake has led to another. We've all been there. That's when we need to impact the environment and make it one that our students can perform in.

In coaching, I'd take an immediate timeout in that situation. Many people think that during that sixty-second timeout, a coach is creating a different tactical plan. Maybe that's true for some, but for me, it's about giving the environment a timeout. Let's take the crowd out of the game and reset the environment to one that we can perform well in.

I have found that this is true for education too. Sometimes kids just need a break. They may have everything in their lives going the wrong way. Their negative momentum is rolling fast and spiraling out of control. Performing well in your class isn't a top priority if the student has home problems or mental health issues, or doesn't know where they will eat or sleep this weekend. We have to call the timeout for them! We have to do something to stop the momentum and build an environment that they can win in.

When to Call A Timeout for Young People

- When you observe consistently poor patterns of academic habits
- When you see a student constantly withdrawn from lessons and their peers
- When you learn that the stuff going on at home is way more serious than your lessons
- When you observe attendance issues. Being in school reduces their negative choices
- When you observe a pattern of poor decisions
- When you observe sadness, despair, and loneliness

Your quirks are a superpower to some young person who needs you. How effective would Aquaman be if he were never in the water? What if the Flash only walked? What if Antman hit a growth spurt? They would not be using their gifts to make the world better. Use your superpowers to offer your students a special champion to kids. You were sent into this profession for a mighty purpose. You were given strange skills. You have a purpose that is specific to you and specific to them. You were made with the personality you have to help young people.

Our students are more like us than not. They are all vastly different just like teachers are. They have strengths, they have weaknesses, and they have problems. And guess what? So do we. So know this: you might be different, quirky, even introverted but there is a student near you that is just like you. And do you know who they would really connect with? YOU. You and you alone have the power to become a champion to that one young person who feels like you do.

One night in 1954, a 12-year-old boy in Louisville, Kentucky, rode his red bicycle to an event at the Columbia Auditorium. When he came out, he discovered that his bicycle had been stolen. The young man was extremely angry and asked where he could find the police. He was told that a police officer was in a boxing gym below the auditorium.

The young man went downstairs and found Officer Joe Martin. He told him that his bike had been stolen and that he was going to whip whoever stole it. The officer told the boy that if he was going to fight someone, he better learn how. The officer owned that gym. Joe Martin took an interest in this young man and gave him boxing lessons, eventually becoming his trainer. The boy was named Cassius Clay, Jr., and would later become not just the greatest heavyweight champion of all time but the most identifiable athlete in sports history. Never underestimate your power to be a superhero to a young person. Our victories are the most powerful ones in any profession.

The Superhero Was Sitting at a Desk

Years ago, I had the privilege of teaching a leadership course for students at our school. It was the first year that I had taught the class. There wasn't much curriculum available, which I saw as a great thing. Instead of complaining about that, I saw opportunities. I did my best to create lessons on winning qualities that good leaders have. The lessons that I most looked forward to were about teaching strategies to bring out the best in others. That was actually a challenge for me. Just giving a motivational speech might resonate for maybe a day. I needed something better.

The challenge was getting them to motivate, not getting them motivated.

So I challenged them and put them to work. I explained that they were going to get their hands dirty and teach each other. I think the best motivators for students are their peers. So what better way to learn this than peer-teaching? Students were given the choice to give a presentation in a variety of ways. They crushed it! Most students made stunning inspirational videos set to music. They really hit the mark, but as good as they all were, one stood out from the rest.

When it was his turn to present, a brave young man walked up to the front of the class with nothing but a piece of paper. He said, "For my presentation, I'd like to tell you about my superhero." And next came the greatest speech I have ever heard...EVER. In his incredible speech, this young man explained that his mother had a terminal illness. Knowing that there wasn't much time left, she spent each remaining day preparing him for the rest of his life with lessons, morals, and advice.

I honestly have no idea where he found the strength to read his speech aloud, but he did and he was incredible. When he finished, I promise you there wasn't a dry eye in the place (especially mine). He touched all of us that day. He nailed it in a way I couldn't have fathomed. Were we motivated? Like never before. I learned two lessons that day. 1. Never underestimate the power of a superhero. 2. Our greatest motivators are at the desks in our classrooms.

3

MISSION CRITICAL

"The ultimate measure of a man is not where he stands in moments of comfort and convenience, but where he stands at times of challenge and controversy."

— Martin Luther King Jr.

Still a senator at the time, a young John F. Kennedy said that in the Chinese language, there is no single word for crisis. He remarked, "The Chinese use two brushstrokes to write the word 'crisis.' One brush stroke stands for danger, the other for opportunity. In a crisis, be aware of the danger but recognize the opportunity." Albert Einstein said, "In the midst of every crisis lies great opportunity." When we go through challenging times it's important to remember that no response is still a response. And then the opportunity is gone.

When you weigh all the factors, the last few years could be considered the most challenging time to teach students in history. If you are a current teacher, chances are that you had a few moments of doubt or reflection. We were already knee-deep in a teacher shortage *before* the Covid-19 pandemic and the social issues that came to the forefront in our country in 2020. There is no sugar-coating it...WE ARE AT A CRITICAL POINT IN EDUCATION RIGHT NOW. Our young people have never needed you as badly as they do today.

The *Wall Street Journal* cited a Labor Department report stating that in 2018, teachers quit the profession at the highest rate in US history. Those numbers have only grown. Roughly 14 percent of all public school teachers are leaving their current school or the profession entirely, according to the latest numbers.

As for the new teachers, there are not enough of them coming. The demand for teachers is projected to grow by at least 4 percent per year, yet among college students, the number of education majors has actually declined for ten straight years and currently is at an all-time low. Minority teachers in education majors are at an even higher crisis level. Even with all the focused attention and money over the last five years, not much has changed. We need our staff to look like our students in schools. They don't. Alarmingly, fifty percent of all new teachers are currently quitting the profession within their first five years. Let that sink in.

The Economic Policy Institute predicts that the teacher crisis could grow to a shortage of 200,000 teachers by 2025. In 2018 that number was at 110,000. I'm petrified to see where today's numbers will climb. So if we know the numbers are this bad, the next logical question is, "Why?" Addressing these issues is critical to stopping this dangerous trend in teaching.

Why Teachers Are Leaving

- Unrealistic and growing time expectations
- Frustrations with leadership
- Lack of support
- Pay
- Challenging work conditions

When looking at various exit polls, it may be surprising to see that not only is money not the top reason given, but it usually ranks between third and fifth. I understand that money will start a political debate that's gone on for years and can be deemed by some to be unsolvable. But when I look at this list, the top three factors *are* solvable with attention and change, not money. So if the main answer is not money, what can we do better? And what specifically is making all these teachers leave?

The number-one reason people give for leaving the teaching profession was the unrealistic time expectations for the job. Not all time is created equal, at least not for jobs. If you were a barista at Starbucks, your shift would at a set time and you would be finished for the day. You wouldn't be expected to stay at the shop for another two hours doing assessments or preparing for when you get back on the clock tomorrow. And I doubt that you would spend hours on your weekend planning for Monday's customers. Imagine having mandatory meetings once a week for an hour on how customers in other states are drinking their coffee when you have a dozen customers to serve. Sounds ridiculous, right?

In 2018, the average work week in the US for a full-time employee was thirty-eight hours. Public school teachers averaged fifty-four hours per week. Of that, forty-three hours were at work and eleven hours were at home. Let's be honest, if you were just teaching your classes, planning your lessons, and grading today's assignments in one day's time...you would not be getting it done in the eight hours that you are paid for. So then most teachers are faced with a "sink or swim" scenario. You end up taking work home each night and on weekends. The problem gets more convoluted when you have to help your own kids with their homework, cook dinner, do dishes, get everyone to shower, and then get them ready for bed. Like a car pushed at 100 mph, this isn't sustainable. Sooner or later the pace will wear you down. The struggle and the anxiety here is real.

We are losing champion teachers, and if we don't listen, it's going to get even worse. Teachers who are already stressed from major time constraints are then often asked to give up half of their planning period for a duty, a meeting, or even a growth opportunity. I always say that time is what you value, expressed. What does that say about us if we spend thirty minutes each way commuting to and from work, eight hours teaching, and then two hours coaching or running a school activity? That's eleven hours a day, and that's a really low estimate for many teachers. That's not including tutoring during your lunch or the hours that teachers spend working at home because a planning period isn't enough time to prepare for all of tomorrow's classes after grading students' work from today.

It's a hard realization, but doing things we love can also rob relationships. Work can rob relationships. Hobbies can rob relationships. Even doing good deeds and helping students can rob relationships. It's easy to lose track of whether your time is balanced, especially when it comes to good intentions. This happens for administrators in education too. Balance must be planned; you can't wing it.

Teaching through Covid brought many time challenges. Every week I saw several people go to Facebook or Twitter to announce they were quitting or retiring early. It broke my heart. And in almost every post, I noticed that they mentioned their frustration with their leaders demanding more time and overfilling their plates as a main reason. It seemed to me to be a tough problem. Leaders were constantly reminding teachers to take care of their health but when would teachers be expected to do that? Faced with tough decisions almost daily, leaders needed to communicate. So more meetings were scheduled. BUT most leaders didn't remove anything from the teachers' plates, they kept adding.

To me, this is where it goes wrong and gets to the disconnected level that stresses employees and takes them to the edge. If teachers are using all of their school time already, you can't add something unless you subtract something. If you are an administrator and want to add something for your staff, I'd ask what you are going to subtract of equal time value.

Leadership "Eye for an Eye" Subtractions

- *Meetings.* If you can't eliminate them by using other communication, condense them. Say what you need to say: WIWO (We In, We Out).
- *Trade time for time.* Trust teachers to flex their time to get the work done. Some might be morning people, afternoon people, or people with situations. Before school or after school...give them a choice to move their work around and work with them here.
- *Borrow them during the day.* Pay a few bucks on a sub for a block of their time to connect with them in a personal meeting. Use the sub for a whole day and

rotate the teachers for as many impactful one-on-ones as you can.
- *Multitask.* Meet with them during a duty like hall time, bus time, lunch time, etc. Maximize the time that's already there.

A Pandemic Problem

During the Covid pandemic, there was no place for a leader to hide. Anybody can lead when it's all going well because there aren't too many tough decisions. The pandemic was *not* one of those times.

The good leaders were tested and the poor ones were exposed. Day after day, the tough problems came without great solutions. In some instances, it seemed like a "Lookup Leader Ladder." By that, I mean everybody seemed to be looking up to the paygrade above them for answers. The teachers were looking to the principals. The principals were looking to the superintendents. The superintendents were looking to the state educational leaders. The state educational leaders were looking up to the governors. It was a mess. Many governors failed to take any leadership responsibility and it became a free-for-all, with each county or district doing their own thing. It felt like martial law.

The education boat was taking on water, and not enough leaders were grabbing buckets. We failed our teachers and students. Teachers either retired early in droves, left education, or just were in a terrible place mentally. The anxiety level of the teachers who were left in the trenches without answers was off the charts.

A December 2020 CNC article reads, "The coronavirus pandemic has put significant pressure on America's teachers. Some have been asked to weigh risks to *their personal health* and *teach in person*. Some have been asked to teach from behind computer screens and *perfect distance learning*. Many have been *asked to do both*. These pressures are taking a toll on teachers across the country." (Emphasis added.)

According to a new report, "77% of educators are working more today than a year ago, 60% enjoy their job less and 59% do not feel secure in their school district's health and safety precautions. Roughly 27% say they are considering leaving their job, retiring early or taking a leave of absence." Only time will tell how much damage was really done to education, but it doesn't sound good to me.

Fifteen years ago, I started teaching at a virtual school as an extra job. I remember being told that the concept wouldn't work and that kids can't learn from a computer. Obviously, the people who told me that were wrong. Later I was asked, "Will teachers become obsolete?" I answered, "The good ones won't." Meaning, good teachers will adapt, grow, and change with the times. Before the Covid pandemic, I noticed a few school systems in our country were starting to make it a graduation requirement to take at least one virtual course. In many instances, change like this was met with strong resistance and bureaucracy.

The Covid pandemic showed us that it is possible to fast-track processes in education and cut through excuses. The urgency that Covid presented allowed us to see that from top to bottom, change doesn't have to take years. It can be done in days if people are committed enough. By now, almost every high school student in the US has taken a class virtually. We may have just created a new way in our country to handle learning on challenging weather days. It's amazing what we can do as a system when we work together.

How We Proceed

Defining and facing problems in education can be a lot like medication. Our complaining should have "Mr. Yuk" stickers on them. We need a little negativity to define a problem, but if we use it more than intended, it can make us sick. We need to identify the problems that are causing teachers to leave our profession. We need to identify the problems that are causing young people to no longer want to become teachers. We need to identify why our teachers across our country are not very diverse. We need to bring attention to problems, apply medication, and cure our ills.

What we don't need is to overdose on negativity by cultivating a toxic attitude. How you view the problem *is* the problem. So focus on solving it, not toxifying your mindset, because that makes you a lesser version of the great teacher you are destined to be.

I have great pride in being a teacher. I've never had any ambition to do anything else since I started. And having great pride in our profession means taking pride in others who are fighting the good fight as well. When I speak to faculties, I love to have the teachers who have been doing it a long time stand up. They deserve my recognition and respect. There is something to be said for any teacher or leader in education who has lasted. They did it, they made it through.

My pride next focuses on the other end of the spectrum, our young teachers. Statistically, not enough of them are staying. They are leaving in their first five years. If we have pride in our profession, do we have a responsibility to help young teachers? Can we, as veterans, use some of the lessons that life has taught us to help them get through their dark days? Can we help them to see through a positive lens and change their mindsets? You might be the only one who stops your work, uprights a young teacher, and maybe changes the path of that young teacher forever. That's really powerful stuff.

Ideas for Helping Young Teachers

- Above all, help them with a positive mindset —often.
- Give them your tradecraft secrets for survival and success.
- Help them with the time expectations, management, and balance.
- Step in. Be a liaison between them and administrators.
- Pay it forward. Do something randomly kind to empower them.

I strongly believe in faith, and my faith has taught me that I do not have complete control. Me worrying comes from a place of me lacking faith as to who is really in charge. Control what you can control and run your own race. Cynicism toward our young teachers is a dangerous influence. The question we should be asking is, "What can we do to help young educators?" You are a great teacher. You have gifts and knowledge. That alone isn't helping them. Let's help them!

Who is the leader in the village? The elder. Why? Because they have experience in all matters. Been there, done that, and seen it before. One thing that comes with age in this profession is wisdom. Chances are you have seen initiatives come and go. You have seen ideas with good intentions, and you have seen ideas with a political agenda being pushed through. You've seen different leadership styles, different assessments, different standardized tests, different students, and different parents.

And because you have seen all that, you have the perspective to give a young teacher what they need while going through it all for the first time. You can be the cure to their anxiety. You can make the challenges make sense. You can tell them how the story ends or at least how to manage it. When I was growing up, I always heard my elders say, *"When I was a kid..."* followed by a story of how they walked to school uphill both ways in a snowstorm. It's easy to have a perspective that things were tougher when you went through them. But for these new young teachers, I'm not sure that's true. I have to believe that going through those first years of teaching with today's challenges is tougher than it used to be.

Imagine if while going through those tough years you had a guardian angel in teaching on your side. Wouldn't that have been great? You can be that guardian angel to a young teacher. First rule, smile every time you talk to them. **EVERY SINGLE TIME.** Let them see you being happy and positive, even though you are sharing the same burdens and frustrations that they are. They need to see that it's possible to feel good, because I promise you, they are seeing teachers that don't. Actions speak louder than words, so shine!

Another way to help is to aid young teachers in relating to and understanding their administrators. Relationships with administrators are many things. They are wonderful, scary, warm, intimidating, and everything in between. You could really help a young person sift through the early career "feel-out" process by sharing what you know about relating to, impressing, and winning the approval of the administrators in your building. Take away their fears and fast-track them to becoming great participants in your school culture.

Pay It Forward to Young Teachers

- Give them time...your time.
- Give them positive visual enhancers (posters, quotes, pictures).
- Give them plans, Including lessons and unit plans.
- Give them a book filled with inspiration and a growth.
- Send random emails or handwritten notes of hope and praise.

Make time each week to stop in their classroom, send an email, give them a fist bump, or just listen to them. In the movie *A Beautiful Day in the Neighborhood*, a reporter is tasked with interviewing Mr. Rogers in between filming sessions of his TV show. The reporter eventually becomes frustrated and leaves. Fred Rogers calls the reporter at a late hour when the report is asleep and explains a life lesson better than I could ever write it. He says, "Do you know what is most important right now? I'm talking to you, so right now you are the most important person to me. Our conversation is the most important thing to me right now."

This is an amazing lesson. The reporter was trying to figure out why this man was so revered by everyone who met him and here was the answer. If you want to connect with young teachers, colleagues, or even students, it starts with giving them a little piece of your time. Mr. Rogers teaches us a powerful lesson to live in the present with the person you are present with. Give them your attention, be interested in them, and show them you value them.

You can help young teachers with the normal doubts in their heads, which come from fear of failure. Set influencers randomly in their life. Imagine a young, budding teacher who is scared and frustrated finding a note from you in an envelope on their desk at just the right time. Or perhaps reading an email loaded with hope, confidence, and inspiration. Wouldn't it be cool for a new teacher to find an uplifting poster or image of wisdom in their mailbox randomly? Just something to remind them that they were made for this...on the days that they might not be sure.

You can also send them a book like *Teachers Changing the Game* (subtle hint) that would inspire, encourage, focus, and add wisdom. Of course there are other great books; the point is to send a young teacher something that will resonate and last for a longer time than an email. Tidbits of motivation like this might just be enough to help these young teachers stay engaged in the same fight that we are in every day. In the end, they are a needed resource in every school. There are assets to their youth that will bring connections to our students, which veteran teachers cannot magically have. Let's stop complaining about the problems in teaching and start addressing them.

An inspired advertising artist named Theodor Geisel had written his first book, entitled *And to Think That I Saw It on Mulberry Street*. It had just been declined by the twenty-seventh straight publisher. He said he was so dejected that as he was walking home, he was contemplating burning the manuscript. As fate would have it, that very moment he happened to see an old friend from Dartmouth named Mike McClintock. After catching up, McClintock asked him what he was holding under his arm. He explained that it was a book that nobody was interested in publishing. Then Geisel asked McClintock what he did for a living, to which he replied, "This morning I was appointed juvenile editor of Vanguard Press, and we happen to be standing in front of my office; would you like to come inside?" Twenty minutes later, Geisel was signing a contract.

That author went on to sell over 600 million books. He had adopted his pen name, "Dr. Seuss," as an undergraduate student at Dartmouth. Geisel was told to stop writing for the school paper after an infraction with drinking alcohol during prohibition, so he created the name "Seuss." Dr. Seuss later wrote a thank-you letter and a book crediting Mike McClintock for redirecting him when things looked tough. Dr. Seuss said, "If I'd been going down the other side of Madison Avenue, I would be in the dry-cleaning business today!"

Not too many people are going to be able to tell you who Mike McClintock was. But that act of encouraging, empowering, and redirecting changed history. Your words have so much power. Your words can change mindsets. Mindsets can change effort and commitment. Effort and commitment can change results. And results can change the world. One single person at a time. Who are you uplifting today? There is a young teacher who could use you.

4
THE LIES

"The truth is still the truth even if no one believes it. A lie is still a lie, even if everyone believes it."

— UNKNOWN

It's not hard to see negativity right now, especially in education. Challenges like virtual and hybrid teaching, budget cuts, teacher shortages, and oversized classes are just a few of the problems that you have probably looked at. When you see challenges in education, which are going to trust...your eyesight or your mindsight?

Your eyesight says that things are helpless and hopeless. But if you have the right mindset and more importantly mindsight, you can see a way to make things work for your students. Instead of being quick to complain or give into the problem, take control of your mind and see yourself as an overcomer. See yourself as a teacher version of a Swiss Army knife, because you are equipped with many tools for many problems.

Our eyesight allows problems and negativity to taint the way we think. Mindsight allows us to have faith in a positive outcome, despite what we see. Our mentality has to be: If you throw me to the wolves, I will come back leading the pack. The pandemic really did a number on morale in education. We are all a little weary from the long, hard fight. I am just as tired as anyone else of seeing the outside influences and problems continue without an end in sight but...I'm not letting them win. I'm just not. I am way too competitive and stubborn for that. So forget the lies that your eyes tell you and look at the facts. Choose mindsight over eyesight.

What Young Eyes Are Really Seeing

- The fact is that our kids are seeing political leaders spit venom at each other daily with nothing off-limits. It has become the norm.
- The fact is that our kids are seeing media coverage of human beings getting hurt, and listening to two sides argue about who was at fault again and again.
- The fact is that our kids are seeing outrageous use of and getting exposure to vaping, marijuana, and opioids.
- And the fact is that our kids are seeing the family mostly as broken today. The place where they were supposed to learn key traits to cope and function in society is damaged.

Eyesight sees these giant monsters imposing their will on our classrooms. Do you mean to tell me that we are supposed to make students feel warm, safe, and like a team with all of that going on? And we are supposed to make them treat others fairly with love and respect when they walk into our buildings, even though many students are not seeing that at home? As sad as this sounds, most states do not have a curriculum built into a school day for kids to face this Goliath. For our young people, eyesight can be overwhelming. This is going to continue to be a long, long, hard fight.

So we'd better buckle up, dig in, and get our mindsight right. Let's make the decision to fight. Let's show up every day with a literal "me against the world" mentality. If your county or district doesn't have a curriculum for this...build your own! The world isn't going to stop coming after our students, so we can't stop getting in front of those bullets. Day by day, issue by issue, we must be relentless.

Fake News

In this new generation of fake and questionable news, we'd better be critical thinkers who question almost anything new or foreign to us as educators. It's a problem when presidential debates are followed by a segment called "Fact Checkers" on national television and our leaders' misinformation is counted by fives and tens. The truth is, people will lie to you. Trends will lie to you. And your eyes, they will most surely lie to you.

So I'm here to tell you something important... DO NOT BELIEVE THE LIES! Do not believe the lies that tell you that you cannot be an amazing leader who people want to follow to greatness, because you can be that leader. Do not believe the lies that tell you that you cannot be the most amazing teacher on this planet, because you certainly can be that teacher. And do not even think about telling me that you "CAN'T" do it yourself because I know that you "CAN."

Listen to me very carefully and never forget these four words: YOU WERE MADE SPECIAL. You were made with hidden talents and skills that not even you have seen yet. And because I know you were made special, I also know that you have the power to be a difference-maker. You have the power to turn a school or a team upside-down with greatness, positivity, and educational awesomeness.

It is so easy for us to be manipulated today for one reason or another. Imagine not doing your best because you were manipulated out of doing something that you knew would enhance, improve, and empower students. Outside influences are everywhere, and not all of them are positive. Some of them crush creativity and momentum when you are attempting innovation. Not all initiatives have what is best for our young people in mind. And the fact is, not all new ideas are good ideas. Be very careful not to buy into the lies. That's right, the lies that come from all kinds of voices that try to persuade you to be less than amazing or make you zig when you should have zagged.

The Savvy Dean

Sometimes we just have to be smarter than the lies—like the story of the savvy college dean. On the night before a final exam, four college students decided to pull an all-nighter and went partying instead of studying. The next morning the four students came up with a plan to get out of taking the exam. They smeared grease and dirt on their clothes and faces and went to see the dean.

They told the dean that they had been to a wedding the previous night and on the way back they got a flat tire. They told the dean that they spent the entire night pushing their car back to campus and asked for an extension. The dean thought for a minute and offered the gentlemen a chance to take their tests in three days. The students were both elated and impressed with themselves.

After studying for three days, the students arrived for the exam. The dean placed each student in a separate room and handed them their exam. When they saw their exam, their jaws dropped when they saw just two simple questions.

1. What is your name? (1 point)
2. Which of the four tires burst? (99 points)

That's mindsight over eyesight!

Do you know who the biggest liar often is? YOU. The fact is that we all lie to ourselves and we do it frequently. You've been selling "fake news" long before we heard that phrase. Lies like "I can't do that" and "I'm not good enough," or "I have no time." The battleground to what you'll accept and what you'll believe about yourself is in your mind.

In any given situation, we are subconsciously offered a choice. We either believe that we *can* do something or we believe that we *cannot*. On the surface, it sounds like an assessment, but I think it's actually a question. And the question is, "Are you willing to do what it takes or not?"

I believe that "I can't" is the most overused response being used by our young people today. Ask a young person to attempt something out of their comfort zone and often you will instantaneously get an "I can't" response. There wasn't a true assessment of the situation, no real thought, just a preprogrammed response that maintained comfort. When listened to over and over, that mentality allows you to sell the lies to yourself. That style of thinking destroys your greatest strengths, like creativity, problem-solving, overcoming challenges, and believing in yourself.

I am a big believer in going outside of your curriculum to build processes and mindsets in our students. I see buying the lies as one of those "must address" opportunities. If your class, your team, or your group is attempting to accomplish amazing things to the best of their capabilities, then it becomes imperative that every member believes in their ability. A good old fashioned "can do" attitude is where overachieving starts.

Educators shouldn't get a hall pass on this either. We are usually very quick to say "I can't" as well. If someone infringes on our time or asks us to do something out of our comfort zone, "I can't" is usually our go-to response. A more candid and accurate response would often be "I am not willing." There's nothing wrong with saying that powerful two-letter word sometimes: "No." Saying that you are not willing to do something is about a decision of what you value as opposed to uttering a lie to others and yourself in saying that you "can't" do something. And that negative thinking is both limiting and contagious.

The real truth about "can't" is that the mind will almost always quit long before the body will. The SEALs call it their 40% Rule. Simply put, when you say that you cannot physically endure anymore, you are actually only 40 percent done. Each year about a thousand talented recruits who have been considered the best of the best make it into SEAL training. The success rate is about 20 percent, which means the failure rate is 80 percent. When a candidate decides they cannot go on any longer, they ring a bell three times to signify that they have chosen to quit trying. When the doctors examine the candidates, they discover that the recruits were at near 40 percent of their limit.

Our minds are either our strongest driving force or our heaviest anchors. Our attitudes control our altitudes. How many times have we all seen a student with limitless potential who is underachieving because of this? Teaching lesson after lesson within my curriculum won't change that. I'm choosing to fight that student's lies. And how do I do that? By using the will of others. Whether it is through a short story, a film clip, or me lecturing about some amazing human being who has taken my breath away, I am sharing it in the hope that it resonates. And I will pound that rock day after day after day.

Nothing makes a young person believe in themselves like a little success does. That's why it is so important to pounce on it when you see it. "Catch 'em doing good," and while you are at it, throw the spotlight on them while announcing it with a megaphone! You making a big deal of the success that they just had will reaffirm the warm feeling they are having on the inside. If a boulder rolls by you with momentum, it won't take much strength to make it go faster. As they say, success breeds success.

As a teacher and a coach, I want to be guilty of overrating my abilities in what I can do for students, as opposed to underrating and selling both them and myself short of accomplishing great things. Self-doubt is a quality that exists in all of us, not just our students. That big, red "I can't" button is always sitting right there staring us in the face, begging for us to hit it in almost every situation. If you want to squelch that voice, start by identifying where it comes from.

Where "I Can't" Comes From

- Patterns. The greatest predictor of future behavior is past behavior. So if I wasn't successful last time, I can't be successful this time.
- Fear of failure. The mere idea of trying something has your mindset focused on the losing result rather than the winning result.
- Insecurities. These are created from feeling inadequate, as if success only belongs to a chosen few, not ourselves.
- Apples to oranges. Sometimes we say "I can't" because "they couldn't." Fact is, you were made special and different in many ways.

The Mind Will Quit Long Before the Body

The mind will usually revert to what it's preprogrammed to think, while the body says, "I am capable, push me." You have a pattern in your life most likely created from your comfort zone. We all do, in most areas of our professional and personal lives. We may teach the same way day after day. We believe that eating breakfast, lunch, and dinner and even eating each meal at a particular time is normal because it's always been that way for us. If you run or walk, you probably have a regular route. Even going to bed and waking up are probably repetitive patterns that you could set your watch by. Life has a habit of preprogramming us, and doing things outside of our norm means risk, even if doing so makes us better. This is a slippery slope because sometimes your comfort sets your limits. It's time to break through your preconceived limits!

I love seeing people shatter myths and rip through perceived limitations. I recently watched an eighty-four-year-old woman from Baltimore compete in a bodybuilding competition. She worked out every single morning at 4 a.m. and never missed a day. So my body is "capable." I watched an incredible young man named Chris Nikic become the first person with Down Syndrome to complete a true, full-length Ironman Triathlon. Are you kidding me? My body is "capable." And I've seen Navy SEALs workout for five and a half days straight with a total of 2 hours of rest in conditions that would make most cry. I might be dragging, but it's a lie to say I "can't" do it because I'm too tired. All we have to do is look around and we can see that there are amazing and inspiring individuals who are doing things that most others say they can't. Their minds are preprogrammed to say "I am capable," and they are the ones we should pattern ourselves after.

Removing Obstacles

Fear is a popular place in our minds, responsible for crushing our dreams and goals. Through different presentations, I have had the privilege to talk to a lot of teachers and coaches in the last couple of years and the more that I listen, the more amazing they are to me. Teachers are filled with incredible ideas and passion. I try to end every conversation by asking them, "What is going to stop you?" The most popular answer...FEAR. So the next logical question is, "What are you afraid of?" That's where I see that fear wears many faces. Fear of failing, fear of not fully committing, fear of what others think, and fear of change.

Fear is absolutely a liar and it will try to paralyze you if you allow it to. The fact is that you *are* good enough. You *do* deserve success in all of your endeavors. It's not a right reserved for the privileged few. Anybody can grind hard, try new things, commit to being a different and better version of themselves. We can all do it. You are capable.

Fear can also come from too much information. One of the terms I learned to use in teaching and coaching is being "just dumb enough." I've noticed many kids do better than they "should" have in a given situation. In talking to them after their great accomplishments, I've often discovered the most amazing thing...they didn't have a clue what they were doing! They didn't know that they should have been scared, should have been nervous, and should not have won or performed well against the competition. They were so clueless that it actually played out as an advantage to them. Intimidation, nervousness, and fear are often learned behaviors from information that we accumulate.

In 2002 I was coaching a talented group of young men. We had just won our school's first regional championship. We won the next game and moved onto the state championship game. Now let me say that in many parts of my life, I am not overly organized, overly analytical, or overprepared. For whatever reason when it comes to coaching, I often am. I believe in preparing our young men for anything they may see and how to respond. So when we reached this big game, I went into information mode. I gave each of our players more than enough data on the opposing team. I practically broke down every opposing player with their strengths, faults, and habits. Heck...I probably even wrote which hand the water boy poured with. I gave each of our players their own copy of the scouting sheet and asked them to study it. On the day of the game, I had our bus driver get us to the stadium four hours early to watch the preceding game and absorb the atmosphere incrementally, thinking that when we took the field, they would be more used to the environment.

We lost that game. Full disclosure, the other team was better. But I felt like our team just didn't play to the abilities that I had seen earlier. The following two years, we were back in the state championship and lost both times. Each year, I felt like we had a tremendous team, but we just didn't play to our capabilities in the biggest game.

After the third loss, I really needed to do some reflecting. I felt great about the level of performance that we consistently climbed to. But when we got to the big game, it was like we were filled with the fear of failure. It was paralyzing. So where was it coming from? The answer was ME!

I did a poor job preparing our players for the moment. I made the stage too big for them to perform. Each time I made those intricate and detailed scouting reports, I subconsciously made our players think and focus on how good the other guys were. In other words, I introduced and exacerbated their fears.

So the next time we made it back to the state championship game, my coaching staff and I vowed to make our players "just dumb enough." Dumb enough to not know that the stage was really big. Dumb enough to show up late to the stadium so that we "did not" absorb the intimidating atmosphere. I wanted us to be rushed with no waiting time. Dumb enough to know that the opposing players were not made out of steel. Dumb enough to know that we should win the game because we just didn't know any better. And it worked. Those players were extremely talented, and at least this time I let their talent shine without the presence of fear.

Other obstacles to identify come in the form of the people who will deter you if you allow it. I call these people "fire extinguishers." They have a variety of reasons for being who they are, but they are rarely encouraging and often know the right buttons to push to put out the fire of enthusiasm and creative thought. Identify them, prepare for them, and overcome them. The incredible ideas that you have are well worth the headaches. When is the best time to put out a fire? Before it gets going. Remember, your body is capable if your mind is willing, so don't let mere words extinguish your fire!

"Fire Extinguishers"

- The "Competitor." Those who see you as a competitor rather than a colleague. It's a competition to them and you know what place they want you to finish.
- The "Status Quos." Some people just don't like change, even if it doesn't affect them. All they will see the potential of more time and work coming their way.
- The "Robots." Some are preprogrammed to say "no." It's our easiest preprogrammed response other than "I can't." The way we've always done it is the way we should always do it.
- The "Chicken Littles." These are usually administrators who are programmed to look for even the slightest sign of something that could go wrong that would impact them. They see the sky falling instead of the amazing possibilities for your school or team.

The truth is that those highly motivated, dedicated, driven, and successful people that we regard as invincible… also hear those same exact voices that you hear. From teachers to celebrities, they hear that noise. They hear negativity like "I can't," they hear voices that say "quit," and they hear the extinguishers just like the rest of us do. The difference comes in what their minds do with those voices.

One tactic taught is to ignore those "Fire Extinguishers." Ignoring that jab or pretending that it will go away is a common and even a mature tactic, but I think it can be detrimental to you too. It's like finding a poisonous snake in your house and leaving it alone because it hasn't bitten you yet. If you have someone or something coming between you and your amazing goal, you need to deal with it in some fashion, even if it's just addressing it in your head. In some way, process the negativity and then you can move on instead of hoping it doesn't come back.

Confront all that teases failure. Engage the source and answer it as if it were a question. Even if the source is my own mind, my favorite approach using that technique is asking the source "Why not me?" You want to be confident in yourself? Use those three words in any challenge. And do you know what I want you to say next? "I am capable and I am willing." History has been created from those words. That is rocket fuel!

I also like to find power from unusual places, like from those taking shots at you. Use the negative shots as fertilizer toward your cause. Do not miss the opportunity to draw strength from those people. If someone throws a brick at you, use that brick to build yourself a firm foundation. And on that foundation, you will build your vision. Not everybody will believe in your vision, but that cannot deter or extinguish you. Stopping what you are doing to engage them is a distraction and probably their intention. Outsmart them. Never wrestle with a pig because you will both get mud all over you but...THE PIG WILL LOVE IT!

It is said that Vincent van Gogh made over 800 paintings but was only able to sell one during his lifetime. Talk about someone ignoring voices and being undeterred! He lived his life in poverty and faced more extinguishers than you or I could imagine. He once gave a painting to a doctor as a "thank you" for his services. That doctor used that painting to cover up a hole in the roof of his chicken coop. Did that stop van Gogh? Not a chance. Van Gogh later did a portrait of a doctor named Gachet. That portrait's value today is between 148 and152 million dollars.

To me, toughness comes in all shapes, and it starts in our heads. That person in the military who defends our freedom 365 days a year, they are tough. The doctors and nurses that went to work during Covid every day, they are tough. The field worker who shows up every day to pick fruit from sunup until sundown to feed their family, they are tough. The funeral employees who comfort those in despair every single day, they are tough. The cancer patient who grinds through chemotherapy, tough as they come. And that teacher that shows up every day for their students despite their frustrations, they are most certainly tough. The first step to toughness is showing up. It's a mentality.

When you feel like your principal isn't being fair to you
SHOW UP ANYWAY
When you feel like you are underpaid
SHOW UP ANYWAY
When you feel like your workday keeps getting longer
SHOW UP ANYWAY
When you feel like you are going to meetings just to meet
SHOW UP ANYWAY
When you feel attacked and not supported by leaders
SHOW UP ANYWAY
When you feel like you're making less of a difference
SHOW UP ANYWAY

You show up because you are a warrior. You show up because you don't do any of this for them, you do it for students. You show up because you are a leader to others and your actions have a ripple effect on every student and team member who knows and respects you. You show up because you have a very specific set of skills that somebody out there is praying to find you with, and you will make a **LIFE-CHANGING DIFFERENCE**. That's why we show up. Bless you.

5

A CHECKUP FROM THE NECK UP

"Experience is a hard teacher because she gives the test first, the lesson afterwards."

— Vernon Sanders Law

Getting older is not as much fun as it sounds. When we are young, we are kind of like credit cards. We have fun with our bodies now and we won't worry about paying for it until later. As we get to a certain age, the physician that we have known since we were kids now demands that we come see him once a year for a dreaded checkup. It becomes an annual assessment of your health and where you are at in that defining moment.

Our careers in education work similarly. The years roll by and suddenly you look around and you are at a number of years. Maybe it's time for a checkup but not a physical one. I think that it is very important after each school year to take an "annual checkup" as to where you are in your career and where you want to be. What kind of year was it for you? How do you think you did? What did you learn that will change the way you operate for next year? These are just a few questions that you should be asking yourself. Just like a doctor, you are going to use the information you have to make a healthy plan when you walk out of the office.

What you cannot do is assess that you are not in a good place and simply ignore it. That will make you an ineffective version of the amazing teacher that you were meant to be. Sooner or later that environment will wear on you and cause you to be bitter, negative, or become the "just for a paycheck, nothing more" employee that we see sometimes in education. A checkup can arm you with information to make a decision.

Yearly Checkup Questions

- How much did I enjoy my job this year?
- What new instructional practices did I try to use?
- Did I make a difference to students who needed a difference-maker?
- Is the environment that I am in a winning one with winning processes?
- Was I a good teammate and would my coworkers see me that way?
- Are my superpowers being utilized, and can they be in this environment?
- What did I read, attend, watch, or hear on my own time to be better at my job?
- What are the three biggest negatives to this job? Can they be fixed or enhanced by me?
- How much of my time in this job was focused on students?

It's Actually Not Your Discipline

We were born with a sinful nature to easily be distracted from our own personal goals and values by looking at others. That "Keeping up with the Joneses" mentality, right? The concept is that more is always better and our appetite for certain things is simply insatiable. Money, popularity, and acceptance are areas where we routinely see this principle at work in our society. We should be focused on our specific goals but instead become distracted by shiny things.

If free money were spilling out of a money machine, when would be the exact moment that you would honestly walk away? You'd have a point, but where would that be and moreover, what would be your rationalization? To me this is a mindset. What do you really value and when will you take control of your thoughts to make them actionable? My morals, strong or weak, would dictate when I walk away. We don't always do dumb things because of our intelligence. Distractions come in a variety of disguises for teachers and students, and before you realized what you were chasing, you changed. This is why checkups are so important.

The misconception is that when we get off-track, we should address our discipline instead of our psyche. In reality, me being off-track is a mindset problem. My mind*SET* was nothing more than being mind*LESS*. Basically, I mentally hit the "go" button but never mentally hit the "stop" button and had no destination in mind. As Lewis Carroll wrote in *Alice's Adventures in Wonderland*, "If you don't know where you are going, any road will take you there." In so many ways, we just go with the flow and never question our thoughts and processes. In other words, we forget to go to our checkups.

How to Catch Wild Pigs

Do you know how to catch wild pigs? They have become a serious problem in parts of the United States. A fence at a wild game reserve was accidentally broken, and a large population of these pigs escaped. In a short amount of time, they ravaged and decimated local farms and ecosystems. The pigs breed fast, eat ravenously, and are difficult to catch because they are cunningly intelligent. Faced with a serious and growing problem, the local mayor offered a reward for any of the wild pigs who were brought in dead or alive.

The day that the wild pig hunting season opened, they had a tremendous turnout. Most hunters entered the woods with rifles, and several attempted to use baited fence traps. But at the end of the first week, they hadn't killed or caught a single pig. The town's mayor was desperate and asked a retired game warden if he would help them. The old man agreed and asked if there was a bonus if he caught more than twenty. The mayor laughed and said, "There are a hundred men a day in those woods and they haven't caught a single pig yet. Sure, I'll give you a bonus." The old game warden said, "Great. Meet me here with a giant storage truck and my check in exactly three weeks."

Word of the old game warden's confidence quickly spread to the others. The next day, the game warden went into the woods with nothing more than a bag of corn and a small, incomplete section of fencing. The others made fun of him, saying, "We are all using corn in our traps and his trap isn't even put together." Every few days the old game warden would go into the woods with a small and incomplete section of fence and a bag of corn. Finally, the night before the three weeks were up, the old game warden called the mayor and told him to pick him up in the giant storage truck the next morning.

They went into the woods with nothing more than another small piece of fencing and a bag of corn. When they arrived at a particular spot deep in the woods, the mayor was confused. There stood a large circular fence that had nothing inside it and was missing one section. The game warden told the mayor to hide behind a tree and watch. The game warden placed the bag of corn in the middle of the fenced off area and walked back to the tree. Moments later more than twenty pigs appeared and began to eat the corn. The old game warden used his last piece of fence and trapped all of them inside.

"I don't get it," the mayor said. "Everybody has traps with corn but the pigs are too smart to go inside. How did you do this?" The old game warden explained that these pigs are like people; sometimes they can't see any harm when things aren't already put together. All you need to do is start with a safe environment and a pleasant distraction. Day by day, the pigs didn't see the fence growing, they just saw the corn.

We do this in our personal lives and we do this as educators. I call this "parking." We assume no control over where we are going, we just chase the corn. We follow patterns without thinking, planning, or assessing. We are subconsciously accepting our outcomes instead of dictating them. When you were new to the teaching profession, you were creative out of your circumstances. You hadn't been around long enough to see all the shortcuts or learn the tricks that might save you time and energy. You didn't have a thick lesson-plan book so you engaged in thought, assessed ideas yourself, and used your creativity to come up with something special. You came up with something specific to you that you believed in.

But as the years go by, more and more teachers stop moving and start parking. Those parking lots are filled with stagnant teachers who still possess so much passion and creativity. We need to motivate each other to start those engines and get them back to what they were meant for. Will Rogers said it best: "Even if you are on the right track, you will get run over if you just sit there." We need to be moving.

Ways We "Park" in Education

- Recycled lesson planning. Teach one year 3thirty times or teach for thirty years?
- Turn Professional Developments into an oxymoron. These were meant for growth and enhancement.
- Closed minds. Teachers decide they can't learn something new because they are too young, too old, too busy, or too stubborn.
- Time in place. We stop accepting new challenges because we are content right where we are.
- Good is the enemy of great. The narrative is why we should challenge students and teachers who are doing just fine.

One of the more frustrating examples of parking is when it is maliciously chosen from a negative mindset. I am a huge believer in being a team. I firmly believe that a well-run school takes two special things: great leadership and team players. The relationship between those two aspects will impact their effectiveness. Imagine telling a student that you require them to turn in their assignments with a new technology platform to which they reply, "No, I'm too old to try that" or "I'm just not good with technology so I am not trying that." I'm pretty sure that you wouldn't accept that answer.

Yet, we see this being done by educators frequently. It's destructive on a few levels. It screams, "I'm choosing not to be a part of the team." I'd ask that individual, "Are you not capable or not willing?" An individual will sometimes fold in a situation where they feel intimidated or anxious. A good leader will deescalate those feelings at the very start by offering any resources necessary as help. After that, it becomes a different problem rather than one of technology.

We are all capable of learning new skills. Whether it's technology or something else, we are not really too old to grow in some way today. If your paycheck was paid to you today with some new technology, I'd bet that you'd figure it out. It's a choice. Always choose to be a team player, because the young teachers are watching. We owe them the optics of trying our best and growing until the day we retire. Let's teach them what perseverance looks like. Take a fear and make it a motivator. It's as simple as changing your mindset.

One thing teachers should be good at is assessing. We spend a lot of time doing it for students. But do you assess yourself? That's another part of a quality checkup. Have you lost some or all of your passion? Do you need to tweak something professionally, or are you too far gone?

Kenny Rogers said it best: "You've got to know when to hold 'em, know when to fold 'em, know when to walk away, and know when to run." One of the toughest things to decide is when and where to move on to a new challenge. Are you where you are supposed to be, using the talents that you have been given, or should you be challenging yourself with some other journey? It's stressful, but it's something I believe you should be mindful of. Like my middle school principal told me at my eighth grade dance, "There's no parking on the dance floor." So let's get moving in some direction. Here is my Kenny Rogers-style advice about possible actions to take when your checkup says you are unhappy.

When to Hold 'Em:
(When to Keep Fighting)

- When what or who you are fighting for is stronger than what or who you are fighting against. The culture and environment are still intact.
- When it appears that you can outlast the negative thing or person that is diminishing your joy for your job.
- When the problem is solvable. Confrontation and communication have to occur before you think about movement.

When to Fold 'Em:
(Reassess and Create a New Plan)

- When the problem that you are upset about is annoying but has little impact on your happiness when resolved. The energy isn't worth the reward.
- When the impact of this particular fight has lost its steam, is played out, and is just a long, unpleasant problem rather than an urgent one.

When to Walk Away:
(It Might Be Time)

- When you feel like you are no longer part of a team with a common interest in serving young people.
- When you are worlds apart with your leader on almost all the most pressing issues and protocols. Strong philosophical differences.
- When you have attacked your serious problem with

your best resolve and efforts and are at an immovable point.
- When the concern for the environment being a winning one isn't there.

When to Run:
(Toxic, Go Now)

- When you are being used as bait in someone else's battle. Self-focused leaders or politically elected people are using you.
- When the environment that you work in has become completely toxic.
- When narratives are protected at the expense of employees doing the right thing.
- When it stops being about students.

If in the end, if you like it where you are, stay. If you are unhappy and the answer is to make a change, then do it. It's normal to have a fear that it might not work out and it's normal to be tentative. But if you have armed yourself with information and the decision is a clear one, then you have to take the first leap. I often have this conversation with high school kids when they are stressed about choosing a college. Somewhere we are taught that this movement is permanent. That's not really true. If they pick a school and after a year it's not a good fit, they can transfer. You can do the same thing or even return someday. You're a great teacher, and who doesn't want one of those?

Finally, I want to share the best piece of advice I was every give with regard to jobs. It came from my best friend and mentor. He said, "Never run from a job. Always run to a job." Ask yourself, are you running from something you are unhappy about or are you running to a better opportunity?

Growth Hormone

The next element to your checkup is assessing if you are still learning. You might be comfortable and in a good-fit situation for a long period of time. You might still be doing a great job teaching, but are you learning? Can you identify people around you right now that you can target for your development? Being good now without attempting growth means mediocrity later.

Sometimes when you say the words "professional learning," what people actually hear are words like boring, waste of time, or hassle. Learning for teachers can come from a variety of sources, like workshops and grad classes, but the ones that I love are the ones that I get to pick. Professional learning shouldn't sound like a trip to the dentist. If it does, then you've had some bad ones. To me, learning about things that I am passionate about is fun, so those are the things I target.

Motivation for an extrinsic credit or a forced sixty-minute agreement between my union and school system is a hard sell. I once dreaded reading and especially writing in high school. My mindset was poor, so my effort was worse, and it was 100 percent my fault. Most of my experiences centered around reading books and passages that I didn't find attractive, and writing was much of the same. It was hard for me to be passionate and expressive when I had no authentic feelings about the material.

Then in my junior year of high school I had an English teacher who would change the game for me. Her name was Ms. Ellen and she was amazing. For some reason she talked to me. She actually had conversations about me, my life, my interests, and even cracked jokes that made me laugh out loud. True story, for the first time in my high school career I was showing up to an academic class early. The culture she set for students was challenging and fun at the same time. She built assignments around her students. She made me read and write creatively by using my passions to get me going. Then she refined me after the passion was flowing to paper. She tricked me into loving reading and writing. I was blessed to have a teacher like that.

As teachers, we talk about how everybody learns differently, but often, our professional developments and faculty meetings are all run the same. It's a challenge when the content of the meeting impacts maybe half of the room. The fact is that we learn differently too. So let's start practicing what we preach. Let's offer professional learning choices instead of mandates. Let's offer different ways to personalize teacher growth experiences to motivate and light our passions for growth.

In the last twenty years the development of the internet, Google, YouTube, online courses, and tons of social media platforms have been launched. If our professional developments and opportunities today look the same as they did twenty years ago, that's not good.

If twenty years ago you had told me that there would be a format where teachers filmed great lessons and ideas and shared them with videos and tips in a place that I could see from my computer at home, I would have screamed for joy. Then, if you told me that at the touch of a button, I could actually comment, question, or send the teacher or expert a direct message...I'd argue that it can't be real. And just when I think it can't get better, I learn that it's free. That's what several social media platforms can offer you. You can follow teachers and teaching organizations on platforms like Twitter and see real lessons whenever you feel like tuning in. You can network and even pick their brains. This is a tremendous way to get better without getting bored.

There is another way we can get better without even leaving our buildings. Try going to the other end of the age spectrum. If you are an older teacher, you can't be twenty-five again. And if you are twenty-five, you haven't ever been forty before.

Obviously, older teachers can help share their experiences and help young teachers grow. That's called mentoring, but it's a mistake to think that the young teachers can't be mentors as well.

I love picking the brains of our up-and-coming young teachers. They have fresh eyes for old problems! Young teachers can offer us the latest and greatest changes to our world too. Most are familiar with the latest apps and communication tools that older teachers haven't been exposed to. And by being new to an environment, they might ask a very important question about why you do things the way that you do…"Why?" They kind of force us to have a checkup. Maybe it's time to look at your process and ask that important question.

Many people may not know that in her early life, Mother Teresa was a schoolteacher. She taught history and geography in Calcutta, India, at an all-female high school named St. Mary's, which mostly served the daughters of the affluent. She taught there for fifteen years, loving the profession, but felt her heart tugging at her when she saw the poor around her. Figuratively speaking, she gave herself a career checkup.

She also believed in professional learning and growth. In 1946, she decided to attend a retreat in Darjeeling, where she made the decision to change her purpose in life. As she began, Mother Teresa took her teaching talents into the slums without supplies. She taught children how to read and write by using sticks to mark the dirt. Her checkup provided her the clarity to serve the poorest of the poor. For the rest of her life, she would change the world in so many ways with her love, her empathy, and her kindness. Maybe your checkup will change the world next? I'm betting on you.

6

TAKE OVER THE MAKEOVER

"The secret of change is to focus all of your energy not on fighting the old, but on building the new."

— Socrates

Ralph Waldo Emerson said, "The only person you are destined to become is the person you decide to be." The man I am today would never be friends with the guy I was years ago. Choosing growth means taking the initiative to become the educator that you want to be. The only real connection that you have to the teacher you were last year is your memory. Be a goldfish and reset your brain every school year.

When I have the privilege to speak to teachers and young people who are looking for hope and change, I find it necessary to be brutally honest at the start. What you need to know is that nobody is coming. That's right, nobody else is coming to check on you. Nobody else is coming to make sure you are working toward success. Nobody cares if you flounder, procrastinate, or fail. Know that nobody is vested in your changing except you. If you want to change and you want to grow, stop waiting on the illusive "Help You" Fairy because she's not coming. You have to help yourself or you live with the consequences. When it all goes bad, *YOU* need to make the next plan, *YOU* need to take the next step, and *YOU* need to be your own motivator. Stop complaining that life's not fair and that you are a victim. Step up and take control of today.

When choosing growth, use caution because not everything that glitters is made of gold. Sometimes things that look and sound good are not in the best interest of kids' growth, or our own. Think of the latest and greatest fails in recent years from your professional developments, or mandates passed down the line from people above your paygrade. Without being too negative, it goes without saying that politics exist in education. When I hear some initiative that makes little sense in a classroom, I always ask, "Where is this really coming from?" That's the first step in the process as I see it. Who wants this initiative done and why?

Things to Ask with New Initiatives

- At inception, where did this come from and who has it been passed down to?
- Who is benefiting from this and who could be hurt as collateral damage?
- Who has done this already and what were their results?
- How similar is the target population to the past population?
- How is this better than what's currently happening?

Much like trends in fashion or the stock market, education can most certainly trend. A few years ago, I remember sitting in an opening year faculty meeting listening to the latest change in our curriculum. The idea was that we were going to completely eliminate the "D" grade. So students could earn an A,B,C, or F. My jaw dropped as I listened. My immediate thought was, "What is this going to change for students?" The way that I saw it, a grading scale was simply a tool to interpret the existing performance and assessments of our students. So this new protocol wasn't going to help me teach any better and it wasn't going to help my students learn more, it was simply changing the way we interpreted their performance. That's not growing anybody.

I listened for an hour and then would subsequently have frequent professional learning sessions selling the concept. Have you ever had someone sell you something you knew in your heart was not for you, but they were so darn good at selling it and so convincing that in the moment, you drank the Kool-Aid? Well that was me. I focused so much on this that I forgot a lot of important things about teaching. If I were really doing my best, I should have been focused on eliminating every grade except an "A." I should have been focused on teaching to the top of the class and elevating the level of *all* students with a standard of excellence. Instead, we misidentified a "D" student as a "C" or an "F" student and failed in focusing our time on addressing the cause. It ended like you would have expected. I was a company man at the time, so I followed the directives in what ended up being a huge failure.

Trends are not always good things in education. Sometimes the latest gimmicks are not really what is best for students. When there is turnover in personnel, the new leader might have tunnel vision about changing everything. They may change administrators, curriculum supervisors, processes, and standards. But if change isn't done properly, it can cause chaos and dysfunction in school systems. If it's broken, I understand the idea to fix it. But the answer isn't always a new innovation. Maybe we are asking the wrong questions. What if the problem wasn't the "WHAT" that was being done before but instead was the "HOW" that was being done?

The Big Four to Wholesale Academic Changes: Quality

I don't care what organization is being overhauled, it all starts right here. Quality speaks louder than words. When attempting to improve the way that our students learn, we must assess the quality of what we are about to roll out. How much does this new initiative improve our students and our teaching? The last system must not have been working well if it's being overhauled now. To me, quality is the most misunderstood of the big four to make our academic changes.

Most people hear the word "quality" and think it translates into, "Is the product good or bad?" I think quality is a lot like beauty...it's in the eye of the beholder. Here's where quality often goes astray. With good intentions, somebody takes something that has worked "somewhere" else for "somebody" else and expects the same results in a different set of circumstances.

We have to identify who we are pitching this change to. That "new thing" might be a really high-quality initiative, but it could be catastrophic for the next group that attempts to use it. Too often, initiatives are rolled out with a "one size fits all" mentality. Learning is specific and it's individual. Even within the same district, schools have completely different cultures. The first thing that most think of when we hear the word diversity is race. That is dangerous thinking to me.

When you compare schools in a system, a statistic on paper could tell you that students in two different buildings look alike. Often, that is very misleading when you walk into a living and breathing school and feel the culture that exists. Our kids are different, regardless of what the stat sheet says. They are not numbers, they are people. We live in a society today where we scream for uniformity, but schools are not meant for that.

If there's one thing that I am sure of after almost three decades of teaching, it is that kids learn differently. We have to tweak and customize these great initiatives to each and every school with their particular students in mind.

Earlier in my career I was asked to co-teach a mathematics class that was designed to help high school students who had failed a standardized test. Truth is, I was terrible with math but my co-teacher was really strong. I focused on helping these students realize how they learn and tried to teach them processes that they could use for success. It was really two classes in one if you looked at what each instructor was teaching the students. The results were really positive, and I enjoyed it. Seeing young people improve each day and get personalized attention, it just felt right. I always felt good when I walked out of class.

Standard

Maybe there was not anything wrong with the last initiative? Perhaps the issue was that the standards were too low, not followed, or not enforced. Not paying attention to the standard after the new "thing" has been implemented is a sure recipe for a disaster. Leaders may spend countless hours preparing to release the next greatest thing in education and once it's active, they relent as if the tough part was over. Standards cannot simply be passed on like a torch.

If you are serious about this, it needs to show in what you are willing to accept. Not calling someone out when their methods are not exactly what you demand is a devaluation of the process. If perfect is the outcome, then perfect is the protocol. Is your standard unwavering or is it a suggestion?

A leader's passion will not necessarily be the employee's passion. That puts standards at risk. If I were running a business, coaching a team, or educating students, I would pay real close attention to this part. I don't care how good your new "thing" is, if you do not spend quality time making sure very specific steps are in place to check standards during and after implementation, you're asking for trouble. You may have success early, but sustaining it will be a challenge and tilt your chances toward failure in the end.

A school system had a great new initiative. They were investing a tremendous amount of money in making their teachers better. They announced that they were paying for their educators to earn three credits offered at any college. The system accounted for the fact that each teacher is different and should have the freedom to grow themselves in areas of their specific content or what they felt were their weaknesses. They made this opportunity mandatory but gave teachers an entire year to do this, citing a concern for their time and busy schedules. This was a well-thought-out, well-developed, and well-funded plan. The local teachers quickly took advantage of this opportunity.

Unfortunately, some teachers took classes that had nothing to do with teaching or growth within their profession. Some took advantage of the situation, taking the easiest, random courses offered for the free credits. The plan was solid, the standard was not. There was nothing in place to measure or stop the misuse of funds, so countless dollars from a plan with great intentions were wasted. By not setting or checking standards, there are no standards.

Implementation

If you are making a big change in education, it had better be implemented well. And by well, I mean with a clear and easy-to-understand system that is sensitive to those who are expected to execute it. If you are replacing one "thing" with another "thing," I would start with your very best sales pitch. If I shove my new "thing" on people with a "just do it and like it" mentality, I might lose the crowd before I even say another word. Again, these initiatives don't always fail because they are bad. Maybe they are good but the person out front implementing them is just terrible at it. Choose the person out front very, very carefully. Seriously, have you been to an event where the person speaking to the group clearly could not relate to or understand their audience?

When I was in the running for the state Teacher of the Year, they had a black-tie gala to announce the winner. It was a first-class event and ran extremely well. Every teacher in attendance was made to feel like a rock star. There were over a thousand people in attendance, and it was even televised to celebrate the moment with others. The night had several speakers, including our state comptroller. Let me preface this next part by saying that I am not into politics and am not making a statement here. Our teachers and unions had been very upset with state leaders related to teacher salaries all year. To say things were contentious would be an understatement.

The comptroller stepped to the podium, adjusted the microphone, and started his speech with an enthusiastic and braggadocious announcement that our state had just moved to one of the top median salaries in the country followed by a specific yearly dollar amount. I doubt if most in the room that night made that median amount. To state the obvious, it did not go over very well with the crowd. When he finished, you could almost see steam coming out of the ears of many teachers, family members, and union representatives in attendance. The mood of the room had changed. This was a case where someone didn't know their audience.

Choose someone who will be amazing at getting the intended audience to understand the benefits in the proposed change. Explain exactly why this is going to be an amazing change worth everyone's time and effort. Sell the purpose and benefits before you sell the change. As educators, we all want amazing things for kids. Explain that and we will all be in this together.

If there are many parts to the change, roll it out in stages. It's like eating chocolate cake. A little will keep me wanting more but too much will make me sick. If you roll out a long, elaborate plan filled with hours and hours of talk, the energy and enthusiasm that you had from selling the change will fade and so will their focus. Whenever possible, use WIWO (We In, We Out).

Ask yourself, what are the greatest setbacks to this new change? Address and de-arm those stressors immediately in stage one. Some will have a voice in their heads focusing on why this is a bad idea, and that voice won't be whispering. Quiet their loudest fears so they can then focus on the benefits.

Immediately after implementation, be sure to provide teachers with resources. There's no more hopeless feeling than being told to do someone else's initiative, follow their directives, and hit nothing but roadblocks and setbacks. Quitting is much easier when it's someone else's idea. So attack those roadblocks with easy resources for teachers to go and get solutions.

Execution

The last consideration to implementing changes is execution. A poor plan is easily executed. Bill Gates says, "Vision without execution is daydreaming." Execution is specific, it's finite, and it's measurable. Whether you are a teacher, a coach, or an administrator, this is where the baton has been passed and it's on you to achieve a result. Change has been planned, implemented and now it's "Go Time." A good idea only becomes a good product with good execution. All the steps leading up to this will have prepared teachers or students for this part.

If this big change requires complete discipline and attention to detail, then structure is the key to execution. If this big change requires creativity from people, then information is key. Arm people with information to make decisions. Give them all the relevant information they could need to get those creative juices flowing and enact the new plan. Information is power and will eliminate a lot of mistakes.

Show what a perfect execution of the plan looks like. Give them something to aspire to. Show them the intrinsic and extrinsic rewards that come with the execution of this great plan. Visualization is a huge motivator and instrument to your cause.

A key to great execution is great focus. Focus on doing each intricate detail well. By focusing like a laser beam on one specific thing before the next specific thing, you will be dialed in with everything that you have. Break down any big task for your students or staff into one small "next step" to focus on and I like your chances. It sounds so simple but it takes commanding thoughts and channeling focus. Focus must be guided and addressed. If you assume they will do it attentively on their own, you are leaving the environment in control.

Legendary Notre Dame football coach Lou Holtz once talked about a lesson he used with his players. Concerned about the mindsets of the young men he was teaching, he wanted them to feel how the mind could be derailed by circumstances and environment.

He placed a wooden two-by-four plank on the ground and asked each player to walk across it to the other side. Successfully, the entire team did it without one single player falling off the board.

Then he took the plank and elevated it to six feet in the air. He asked his players to again walk across the plank to the other side. This time, over 50 percent of his players fell off. It was the exact same plank with the exact same dimensions. So why did they fall off?

Focus. When I say that I don't mean they lacked it. None of them wanted to fall so I'm sure that they were focused. With the board on the floor, the players felt safe, the focus was on the task, and performance soared. But when the board was elevated, the change in comfort changed the focus. Funny how one variable can do that. The players were focused on not falling. The players' mindsets were focused on failure.

When attempting new initiatives, make sure teachers can spend time on their real focus, not distractions or failure. Show me how I can make a young person feel better or achieve more and I'm in!

Taking that lesson to our students, if we build an environment that they feel safe in, we can improve their focus. Improved focus leads to better execution. What height is their plank at? Think about the young man or woman in your class who has a tough life. Divorce, abandonment, or abuse are easy detractors from their focus. My lesson might be the same to each student but their safety levels within my same environment are not. Relationships matter. I need to have a great relationship with that student to set an environment conducive to focus and execution.

Four Steps to Changing Yourself

I am a believer in simplifying things when possible. When we complicate things with too many rules or too much instruction, I think we take away the individual's creativity in most given situations. By creating just a few rules or giving a few fundamentals, we allow our stars to shine. That holds true in teaching, academics, athletics, and even in the school play. When it comes to changing ourselves, I think we can do it in four simple steps.

1. Unlearn your limitations. Learned behavior is a result of experiences. You were not made inadequate, you learned it. You were not made negative, you learned it. You were not made with limits, you learned them too. The first step in changing yourself is embracing that you have no limitations, and you can change anything that you firmly direct your mind to change. The only reason past behavior is the best predictor of future behavior is because people do not understand this key concept. Choose to change patterns.

Most people, young and old, want to change their behavior. They just need some help with their plan and their process. Performance is measured in the present. A wrong answer or a wrong choice on another day has no real connection to right here and now. We do not always think like that. If a student did not do well academically or behaviorally yesterday, there is no script that has been read or rehearsed that they have to repeat any behaviors today. If you are not thrilled with a facet of your teaching performance, focus on the fact that you are not retired yet. Disconnect and break those chains. Move forward and keep going. The only time we should look back is to see how far we've gone.

Create affirmations that you say out loud related to your desired change. Don't let that negative whisper in your head conquer you; instead dominate that whisper with a real voice speaking out loud saying something positive related to your change in progress. Create an alter ego that goes by another name. For example, "I'm not Joe Smith, I am Mr. Smith and I am not human. I am capable of extraordinary things that others can't or won't do. My energy is limitless, my mindset unshakable, and I can solve problems that nobody else can." Stop roadblocking yourself. You have no limits! No one else is coming, so do it yourself.

2. Redefine problems. Have the uncanny ability to see someone else's narrative at all times. Look at a problem with fresh eyes. Understand where it came from and how it specifically impacts you. Everyone else's emergency doesn't have to be your emergency.

Next, see your options. Usually, you have three choices when facing a problem. Accept it, change it, or complain about it. Accepting it is letting the problem beat you. Complaining about it is worse as you allow it to beat you and train your brain to be negative and ineffective. Which leaves changing it. Ask yourself: What opportunity exists for me in this challenge? Can I learn from this? Can I grow from this? Maybe you didn't solve the problem but you worked on having a good process or not being a procrastinator, and you won the battle in your mind to not be negative or let this problem define you.

3. Stop saying negative things. Make a pact with yourself that you will not say anything negative out loud today...nothing. See if you can do it. Successful? Try it again tomorrow. Watch how this impacts your behavior. Negativity is a lot like smoking. It's one thing for someone to have a negative habit, but breathing it out is just as harmful for anyone else around it. The answer is to stay away from it. Win your thoughts. You have to control them not the other way around. Be aware and on the lookout every minute for negativity, and have no part of it. When you say it out loud, you hear it and process it again. Stop sabotaging yourself. Nobody else is coming so do something about that!

4. Stop giving value to those attempting to devalue you. If someone was punching you, I doubt your response would be to punch yourself as well. You wouldn't hurt yourself just because someone else was trying to do it. But that's what we do when someone takes a verbal shot at us or disapproves of us in some way. It's illogical. Nobody is coming to make sure your value stays strong when others don't like you. Dominate your thinking and be in control of your self-esteem. You have value and you were made perfect. Someone not approving of you can only take value away if you give it to them. In my opinion this is the number-one biggest cause of teenage depression and anxiety.

If I showed someone an original Honus Wagner baseball card, I think most would say that it is ugly or unattractive. It is dull in color and perhaps looks more like an old painting than a shiny baseball card. Most would criticize it. And if they did, it would still be worth $3.12 million dollars. If someone has a negative opinion of a material object, it does not lower the object's value. Stop letting people do that to you. Your value is your checking account, not theirs. Let them think what they want and keep your account full anyway.

There is a Japanese proverb, "Nana korobi, ya oki" which translates into "Fall down seven times, stand up eight." If you are going to try to do something different or new, failure will be a common deterrent. Focus on this simple proverb. Say it out loud at the discovery of a problem. Be relentless toward building something better.

The Secret Scroll

There was a rumor among teachers at Franklin High School that an actual genie in a bottle existed and was found in the hallways from time to time. Supposedly this genie was the keeper of the "Secret Success Scroll" for teaching. One day a frustrated and dejected teacher named Sarah was headed home after a hard day of teaching. Before she got to the exit door, Sarah saw an oddly shaped bottle and picked it up. She took the lid off and out popped the fabled genie.

"Sarah, you get one wish related to teaching and nothing more. How may I help you?" said the genie. Sarah thought for a long time. She recalled all the teachers that claimed to have seen this genie and then put the pieces together.

"I know that John found you a year ago and in the past year he has been the most positive teacher that I have ever seen. He's happy, loves his job, and is a light for all," said Sarah. "I also know that Mary Jo found you two years ago, and in that time she has changed from a lazy teacher into someone who is always working hard to make others better," Sarah continued. "And I'll just bet that you are the reason that our science teacher Larry has transformed himself from a person with no confidence into an unstoppable advocate for leading others."

The genie asked Sarah for her one wish again to which Sarah replied, "For my one wish, I want to read the Secret Success Scroll for teaching." The genie granted Sarah's wish and presented her the scroll. On the outside of the scroll were words that read, "Inside this scroll is the hero that you need to find to unlock greatness." Sarah opened it and beamed as she read five words: "No one else is coming." They were written on reflective paper, and she saw her own image.

7

MODUS OPERANDI

"We are what we repeatedly do. Excellence, then, is not an act, but a habit."

— Aristotle

Roman emperor and philosopher Marcus Aurelius said, "Your life is what your thoughts make it." Meaning, you have a choice as to how your story goes. We often have this idea that greatness is reserved for a chosen few or that it's in the rare DNA of the lucky but not in us. Some are told they are destined for greatness, but the people I bet on are the ones who tell themselves that. Greatness is really just a combination of a winning mindset, an effective plan, and a strong work ethic. That's a recipe that works for teachers, students, schools, and teams.

In 2018, the University of Virginia men's basketball team had a historic regular season with a record of 31–2, playing in arguably the best conference in America. They were rewarded with the number-one overall seed to the NCAA tournament. Their opponent in their bracket was the lowest ranked team, the University of Maryland at Baltimore County. Virginia was over a twenty-point favorite to easily win the game.

UMBC shocked everyone when they won the game by twenty points, in what could be considered the greatest upset in college basketball history. The players and coaches of Virginia had to endure a painful media storm, criticism, and negativity for an entire year.

The very next season, the University of Virginia won its first national championship in its school's history. And it wasn't easily handed to them. Virginia was losing in the final f seconds of each of their last three tournament games and somehow won all of them, including two in overtime. Their head coach was Tony Bennett, a humble servant leader who believes in doing basic things with a habit of excellence. After they won the championship, UVA president Jim Ryan offered Coach Bennett a raise, to which he responded, "I have more than I need. I'm blessed beyond what I deserve," and then turned the raise down. Coach Bennett would also donate $500,000 toward an initiative for current and former Virginia basketball players toward career training for life after basketball.

This is a leader who values excellence from himself and as a result gets it from his players. How we carry ourselves as teachers creates culture. Culture creates environments that our young people can either flourish or flounder in.

Winning Habits Every Day

If you want to change a culture...aspire to greatness from yourself while inspiring greatness from others. Take no shortcuts and embrace doing the things that others see as mundane, trivial, or beneath them. Someone is always watching and you alone control what's on that channel. Show coworkers that you do not mind attacking tasks that others in your culture may deem "not their job." For in that grind is the so-called secret to greatness.

Imagine seeing your most established teacher scrubbing something off the floor, cleaning desks, or stopping in the middle of a crowded hallway to pick up someone else's trash. That sends a message that you value your building and care about the culture. Be vigilant in not only restraining from complaining, but being active in finding answers. Instead of saying, "That's not my job," what if you said nothing and attacked a problem that wasn't even yours? That is somebody special. That is somebody with excellence.

If you want to be an excellent teacher or leader, you have to have goals. I don't know any great individuals that say, "You know, my goal this year is to just be as good as I was last year." That's not excellence. Goals allow us our first glimpse at the excellence that we seek.

But goal-setting is actually the easy part of the process. That's mostly about wanting good things to happen for yourself and who doesn't want that? My question to you is, do you really want it? I mean, do you want something so bad that you will become obsessive about it? Have you ever taken your temperature to see exactly how badly you want your goals?

If you feel that your long-term goal is mighty and well planned, then your short-term goals should be even better. Typically when I engage high school aged students about a lofty long-term goal that they have in life, I often find that they actually spent some time developing their mighty goal. But their short-term goals typically are inadequate and not well thought out. It's the short-term goals that are responsible for taking a step forward each and every day so you don't lose sight of your destination…just win today.

Nothing long-term is quickly attainable. Meaning, that's a whole lot of discipline and motivation and for a long period of time, without a "feel good" result. So where can you find gratification and motivation along the way? It's in the discipline of those short-term goals. I'm nobody special, but before I would teach a single class, I would have a tablet filled with today's goals to win before I went home. Without them I would probably be self-centered, lazy, negative, and unproductive. Try writing short-term goals at the start of every day and just watch how much you can get done.

Daily Short-Term Goals to Win Your Day

- Which students can I focus on serving or growing a relationship with?
- Which faculty member in our building will I uplift today?
- What ten-minute reading, training or video-based content can I put my eyes on today?
- What task that absolutely sucks will I do today to discipline, humble, and focus myself?
- What health benefit will I receive today because of my nutrition and exercise?
- What one negative habit will I focus on eliminating today?
- What did I do for ten minutes to gain ground toward my long-term goal?

A bright and ambitious student once shared his long-term goal with me. He was a senior and said he wanted to make a million dollars in the next year. The next question I asked him was, "What are your short-term goals?" He gave me the textbook answers that you would expect from anybody not serious about a goal. Hard work, dedication, blah, blah, blah. I explained to him that I could use his same short-term goals to be a pizza deliveryman. There was nothing specific or measurable about anything that he said. With that kind of thinking, dreams are sure to fail. It might sound mean, but I was being straightforward with him out of love.

I got my calculator out and asked him, "Have you really thought about what this means? To make a million dollars in a year, you will have to make $83,333 a month, $19,230 a week, and $2739 a day on average. There's your three biggest short-term goals." His response was, "Wow Coach, that's not realistic." Short-term goals allow you to track progress daily.

It's very easy to confuse long-term goals with unrealistic dreams. To me, a long-term goal is something mighty yet attainable. Something possible but not always probable. That's where I see the beauty in this. When I hear someone say, "He's a dreamer," that's negative to me. Dreams are what we have when we are asleep and are fantasies. A vision, however, is a mighty and powerfully positive thing.

In his 1946 book *Man's Search for Meaning*, Viktor Frankl said, "Everything can be taken from a man but one thing: the last of the human freedoms—to choose one's attitude in any given set of circumstances, to choose one's own way." Frankl tells of his experiences in a Nazi concentration camp in World War II. He believed our thoughts were so powerful that they could control our health. He noted that when victims in the camp lost hope, within seventy-two hours they would die. He noted that those that had a positive view, like visualizing who they were fighting for, had high survival rates.

Trevor Moawad has been named one of the world's best "Brain Trainers." He has worked with CEOs, teams, and athletes at the highest level. In his book *It Takes What It Takes*, Moawad says, "Negativity affects you negatively 100% of the time." One of his greatest tactics in working with teams is to simply disallow any negative talk out loud. That's it; it is both simple and brilliant. If it's hot outside, you can think about it, but you can't say it out loud. His rationale: "If somebody says something negative out loud, it's ten times more powerful than if they think it. And negativity is 4 to 7 times more powerful than positivity." Think about the possibilities in education where we could use that to influence our students, our teams and our environments!

See It and Believe It

Done right, visualization is actually a form of preparation. I think most people hear the word "visualization" and think it means seeing a finished goal. It can certainly be used like that but by itself, that's not much more useful than a daydream. It's great to see positive things happening. That will give good vibes and contribute to high morale. But by itself, seeing the finish isn't really preparing or improving me to execute a plan for success. If you want to use visualization to make you better at something, the key is using real information, real data, and real processes as part of your visualization.

James Nesmeth was a prisoner of war in Vietnam. He spent seven long years in a cage that measured four and a half feet long by five feet tall. Let that sink in. He survived in what could only be called inhumane conditions. When he was released, he was asked how he survived. He said he used visualization every day. He visualized himself golfing at his favorite local golf course. But what I found interesting about his visualization was that he wasn't just seeing himself having a nice day at the country club. He used specific information and data. He played all eighteen holes each day and was a stickler for the small details in each vision.

He would envision taking a specific club out of his bag, gripping it until it felt just right in his hands, and then taking two practice swings with the club each time. He envisioned taking his stance for each shot and then saw himself take his backswing, feeling the ball at impact, and watching its shaped flight. Small details like parking his golf cart, wiping the dirt off his clubs, and even taking cold sips of water were part of his vision for each hole. This continued until he heard the rattle of the ball in the cup after he made the putt at the end of each hole. James Nesmeth was using every detail of information that he could remember to create a realistic visualization.

The most incredible part of the story was that James Nesmeth's average score at that course was in the mid to low nineties before he left for Vietnam. Without touching a club for seven years and living in unspeakable conditions, he shot a personal best score of seventy-four on his first round of golf. He bettered his score by twenty strokes! Envisioning greatness is a weapon we can all use for ourselves and our students.

When I hear someone tell me about a new idea for teaching, I always ask the same question: "What does it look like in *my* classroom with *my* students?" And then I envision that as they are talking. I'm using their idea with my personalized visualization and information.

Do you remember US Airways Flight 1549? Maybe you remember it better as the "Miracle on the Hudson River"? On 15 January 2009, an Airbus 8320 airplane that had just taken off from New York City's LaGuardia Airport struck a flock of birds. The plane's engines were disabled, which left the aircraft with no power. Suddenly the pilot would be forced to make a life-or-death decision followed by an attempt to execute his plan for saving 155 lives.

Captain Chesley Burnett "Sully" Sullenberger decided his best option was to attempt to land the airplane on the Hudson River. Talk about a mighty goal with unbelievable pressure. Our country watched live as all 155 passengers and crew survived the incident. When asked how he did it, Captain Sullenberger said, "One way of looking at this might be that for forty-two years, I've been making small, regular deposits in this bank of experience, education and training. And on January 15 the balance was sufficient so that I could make a very large withdrawal."

He had been prepared for that moment. His vision, planning, and preparation saved lives and he became a hero. What mighty goal are you preparing for? What do you envision that is amazing for your career? What special thing do you see happening for your students? Plan it, see it, and accomplish it. Do not just drift day by day. You deserve so much more than that and so do your students. Get busy dreaming!

Relating to People

Another trait of excellence for teachers and for students is relating to other people. How can anyone lead if they cannot relate to others? And I don't mean people who look like you, talk like you, think like you...that's easy. A winning environment is a team environment. I want my students feeding off each other in a good way. When one student has momentum, I want the others to get a piece of that. When one student has an inspiring moment, I'd like them all to share it. Anything that is positive, energetic, empowering, or enhancing...should be shared as a team, like sharks feeding. If one of us gets better, we all get better.

Teaching students virtually really made me reflect on how much I value what students bring to me each day in energy, life, and passion. I know that we are the ones who are always supposed to always be "ON" and bring the energy to our students. But after just a few classes, I noticed that some students who never missed school before were now missing classes. I also noticed that some students chose not to have their cameras on, while others just didn't interact with the same energy as they did when we were all together in a classroom live.

I kept asking myself, "What is off here?" I mean, I mostly had the same parts that felt great every day. I was there. They were mostly there. So why wasn't the energy anywhere near the same level? Why couldn't I replicate the authentic feelings of trust, openness, and quality communication? And then I looked on my wall and reread one of my all-time favorite poems. I'm such a nerd that I often load the walls around me with positive propaganda so I can strategically see it on days like this.

The Law of the Jungle

Now this is the law of the jungle, as old and as true
    as the sky,
And the wolf that shall keep it may prosper,
but the wolf that shall break it must die.
As the creeper that girdles the tree trunk,
the law runneth forward and back;
For the strength of the pack is the wolf,
and the strength of the wolf is the pack.

— Rudyard Kipling

And there it was! We were not really a pack but a group of individuals in our own homes meeting through technology. That took away some of the authentic feel of our pack. We were just single wolves not using the Law of the Jungle. We were not a team working together socially or educationally. We had no idea what was new, interesting, problematic, or great in each other's lives.

Is this what it feels like in classrooms where the teacher is the authoritative dictator who lectures every day and makes it the students' responsibility to learn? I remember the feeling I had in college with a class or two like that. I didn't really know anybody in the class. I never spoke. I just showed up, took notes, and went home every day. That was "Lone Wolf" teaching and I'd argue that many students like me underachieve in those environments.

Characteristics of "Lone Wolf" Teaching

- The teacher is always at one level and students are at another. Never the two shall meet.
- Old-school library environment. Silence at all times.
- One-way communication: I talk, you listen.
- Students engaging in peer-teaching, interacting, having input, and differentiated learning are not welcomed.
- Accomplishments, victories, and momentums are not celebrated.

I've shared that Law of the Jungle poem with many of the teams I have coached in the past and I have even had them recite it together before games. I have also used that poem as an opening for classes that I felt needed a better sense of comradery. I'm a big believer that a functional group working together can achieve excellence. Our "pack" needs an environment that says "we are in this together" and has an "all for one and one for all" mentality. If I cannot carry the torch of greatness today, maybe one of my students can supply the mood or energy that we all need to attain excellence.

To me, the Lone Wolf teachers miss the greatest lessons, the ones our students have to offer. If you have thirty students in your room, that is thirty stories waiting to be heard. Each of them possesses questions that we are qualified to answer. Each of them has intriguing stories waiting to be heard. They also have lessons that could positively impact the other twenty-nine students. If there is a negative, that can be a lesson waiting to be discovered. This is why relationships are so important as a leader. If you do not possess a good relationship with these students, they will not be inclined to share. But if they feel part of your team, part of your pack... now you have something special!

Lone Wolf teaching is not communication between the teacher and the student. It is a one-way street as far as communicating goes. That's sad to me because I don't know if anything is more important when building relationships. It's the reason I come to work every day and the reason that I feel great when I go home.

You have winning traits and superpowers as an educator. Those winning traits help you to strive to achieve excellence. But maybe you have been doing this for years now. Add to that some negativity around you in education and perhaps your passion has taken a hit, if only for a moment. We have all been there, including me. The students we have in class today deserve our best. These kids deserve the same amazing you as kids twenty years ago got. When I catch myself allowing negative circumstances to impact my thoughts, I like to remind myself of the "Master Carpenter" story.

The Master Carpenter

There is an old story about a master carpenter who had been building houses his entire life. His boss loved him because he was a dedicated and passionate carpenter who always performed well beyond expectations. But like us as educators, he had been doing this a while and was losing a little steam. He informed his boss that after all these years, he was finally ready to retire.

His boss was sad to see him retire but was grateful for a lifetime of outstanding service. He asked the carpenter if he would build one last house for him. The carpenter agreed and built that one last house. It was apparent that he did not have the full passion that he had throughout most of his career. He took shortcuts, lowered his usual standard of excellence, and even used substandard materials, which he would never have done in his past.

Finally when he was finished, his boss approached him and handed him a key. "What's this?" said the carpenter. "This is your retirement house," his boss said with a smile. The carpenter would be reminded all his remaining days of the one job he did without passion.

. . .

That story is a great reminder to me. No matter what problems are around me or frustrations I may have...I am responsible for my passion. I am responsible for my thoughts. Nobody can take that away from me unless I allow it, regardless of what they do. Excellence occurs from the habits I have and the thoughts that run through my head. That's all that I can control. President Roosevelt said it best:

> "It is not the critic who counts; not the man who points out how the strong man stumbles, or where the doer of deeds could have done them better. The credit belongs to the man who is actually in the arena, whose face is marred by dust and sweat and blood; who strives valiantly; who errs, who comes short again and again, because there is no effort without error and shortcoming; but who does actually strive to do the deeds; who knows great enthusiasms, the great devotions; who spends himself in a worthy cause; who at the best knows in the end the triumph of high achievement, and who at the worst, if he fails, at least fails while daring greatly, so that his place shall never be with those cold and timid souls who neither know victory nor defeat."

8

RENT'S DUE

"Success is never owned, it's rented and the rent is due every single day."

— UNKNOWN

A reporter who was watching Mohamed Ali train was amazed at his conditioning and asked him, "How many sit-ups can you do?" Without hesitating Ali said, "I don't know. I only count when they get tough." When things are at their toughest, we find out our real capabilities. Throughout history, people have accomplished unimaginable things because they simply had to. The results of failing were so serious that failure could not be an option. Suddenly we can go to a whole new level of focus that we didn't even know that we had. Imagine if we could always be at that level.

I like to call this our "rent's due" mentality. When your back is up against the wall and you have nowhere else to go, you find a way to do whatever it takes to pay the rent. If you want to be a great teacher having a "rent's due" mentality will change you. It's about having a relentless will to do your very best at what you do and to do it right now. It's about being available to any student who needs your help, anytime. When your rent is due, there is no time left for procrastination. It's time to be our best now.

Putting things off until later is not a winning habit. Picasso said, "Only put off until tomorrow what you are willing to die having left undone." If you want to find a way to *not* accomplish your goals, you cannot do much better than to possess this poor trait. Lacking urgency toward getting things accomplished is a highly contagious losing habit. Identify it in your life and eradicate it immediately before it spreads.

Getting things done and working with focused urgency are winning habits, but they don't just magically appear in our DNA as educators. This is a problem with our perception. When given a job or a task, how do you perceive it? Usually your mind will want to perceive it as negative, another distraction, or an unpleasant effort. Right there is where you lost the battle before it even began. But when your "Want to" becomes your "Got to," that's when you have something special.

How many times have you seen a student underachieve all semester until there is almost no time left? Then one night, they are amazingly able to turn in more assignments than they've done in a month. Their rent was due. It has frustrated teachers for a hundred years. If only that student had worked with that mentality all the time, they might have been an "A" student.

What if you could change the way you perceive the problem? Imagine taking pride in being a problem-solver and hitting things dead-on, any time you saw them coming. Grow yourself to embrace the struggles in these little battles. In a twisted way, you can take pride that you are wired differently. When everyone else is running away from the problem, you are running to it. You become a "seek and destroy" leader instead of a cry and complain educator. Hit tasks with urgency and watch how it empowers you, grows you and makes you more productive.

What Will You Accept?

Another aspect of having a "rent's due" mentality is having a high standard with tasks. It doesn't just mean finishing fast. It means working with urgency and purpose. Working without purpose is just doing things without heart and passion. You need passion! You can't fake it, and without it you can't be any good at what you do. It's the single most important ingredient in building yourself back to where you belong. Regardless of the subject area, taking a young person to a better level is something we can all draw passion from.

At what height do we set our own bar for success and at what height do we set it for our students? If you set a bar too low, you reward mediocrity, and if you set the bar too high, your unrealistic goal could discourage jumping over that bar and instead promote ducking under it. I am a firm believer in setting and having winning standards. Good is the enemy of great. How you do something, is how you do everything. The standard is the standard. Every day you either enforce or ignore standards. Your standard might be mediocrity or it could be excellence. What many years of teaching and coaching have taught me is that wherever I draw the hard line as a leader, students will go.

If I asked you, "What are you willing to accept from your students?" I'm guessing that most of you have a high standard for them. I doubt that you make most assignments pass or fail. Those students are your passion, and you care about how they develop. If you have a low standard for them, that's exactly where they will meet you.

I have come to realize that most students do not yet have a great standard and therefore do not have a great process. If they turn bad work in and I reward them for that, then I just taught a false lesson that is sure to repeat itself. If I am not willing to accept 99 percent, they will eventually meet me at 100. Standards and processes are like oxygen and carbon dioxide: breathe one in, and the other is bound to come out. Our standards shape their processes.

Our Standards Impact Their Processes

- A low standard actually can have a purpose of small victories. It can open the door to learners that have shut down and disengaged. Step one with these kids is showing up and engaging. We can't shape them until they physically do any work, even bad work. Build them up and reinforce the process of doing work.
- Mediocre standards could be used for the student who just started working. Pick the most important things to address instead of all of them at this point. Overwhelm them and their coping mechanism is quitting. Play it out for the long haul.
- High standards are for the students that you assess as having the capability of excellence. Most will fall in this category. Draw the expectation line very early and fight hard battles until the behavior is corrected.
- Impeccable standards are for the students who were born special. Their gifts can teach false lessons related to work ethic, so hammer them over little

things to teach them that good is the enemy of great.

So we have high standards for our students, but do we have the same standard for ourselves? What are you willing to accept from yourself? How high is your standard? Is your standard "finished" or is your standard excellence? Is your standard "almost" or is it "completely"?

When I was a young boy, I remember walking with my little brother across a farm to a local pond to go fishing. Every day we passed an electric fence. I always wondered what would happen if I touched that fence but fear always stopped me. One day, I was smart enough to do what any older brother would do in that situation...I told my little brother to touch it. After I assured him that it would not hurt, he completely grabbed it instead of simply touching it, and as luck would have it, the current was on. The electricity made his hand muscles contract so he couldn't let go of the fence. The purpose of the fence was to keep animals in and me out. I was curious so I tested that system. Once I witnessed that lesson, I was never curious about that fence again.

Our students are curious too. They test systems and standards daily and so do we. It's just what we do. When students go off to college, they usually learn fast who the professors are that have the reputation for grading lightly and giving the least amount of work. They are looking for the easy standard, and they will go through the effort to get the answer.

If I am getting heart surgery, I sure hope my doctor doesn't have a low standard. If I am telling my students that they are fine with a 3.1 GPA and the college of their dreams requires a 3.2, I am hurting them.

Having a high standard is daily commitment. It's much easier to have a low standard. But it is a "pay me now or pay me later" scenario. Some battles need to be fought. That is how lessons, growth, improvement, and development are made. Is it fun to look into the mirror and admit our faults? Of course not, but until I hold myself to a high standard, I will be stuck at the same standard. It's not fun to tell a student that what they did was beneath their capabilities, but you either endorse their low standard or you address them.

Where Low Standards Come From

- Laziness. Growth requires energy, maintenance doesn't.
- Avoidance of conflict.
- A misunderstanding of the impact in doing nothing when something needs to be addressed.
- The past. The greatest predictor of future behavior is past behavior.
- Leadership. If you have no enforced standard from a position of authority, then there are no standards.

When you are in the middle of a "rent's due" moment, it's stressful and it's a struggle. But keep in mind that it is our struggles that make us stronger. I don't know many educators who haven't struggled or suffered in recent years. Within that suffering are defining moments where you somehow found a way. Teaching through Covid provided loads of those moments. But you did it, you answered the bell. You found a way. And now some things just don't seem too scary anymore.

I am probably the world's absolute worst gardener. I am like the Grim Reaper to anything planted. I have not had much success with any plant that I have ever tried to grow. I think it's because I get so busy, I just don't give the plants the attention that they need. One day, I decided things were going to be different and I planted a tree.

I was committed this time and if I do say myself, I was pretty amazing to this tree. If the instructions were to water it two times a day, I did it five. If I was asked to feed it nutrients every month, I did it every week. A few years went by and this tree really looked great.

One night we had a ferocious storm. I went outside the next morning and noticed that my tree had been blown over and was lying on the ground. Not another tree in the neighborhood had been knocked over. I was fired up. I called the nursery where I had purchased it years ago and told them what had happened. The man on the phone said, "Did you water and feed it?" I said, "Religiously! That tree had the most water and food in the neighborhood." He gave me an "Ahaaaa" and said, "Go measure the roots."

When I told him how long they were, he explained that they were one fourth as big as they should have been. He explained that when you overwater and overfeed trees, they won't develop strong roots. By giving it less help and making the tree struggle a little, the tree works hard and grows its roots deeper, making it less dependent on me doing everything for it.

Never ask for an easy life. It's not likely and it will change your standards. If we just give students easy A's, are we really helping them? Do we challenge students to work for their answers and to develop a solid process that they can use in life after high school? What did a student learn if they gave a mediocre effort but got an outstanding grade? You just taught them that mediocre will get them rewarded. Is that how their boss is going to do it in a few years? I've not heard an owner of any company ever say, "Thanks for giving me a mediocre effort, here is a large bonus." It's not going to end like that.

I'm not a fan of everybody getting a trophy once they are old enough to understand processes. It's arming young people with a system that is doomed to fail. To me, this is where many people blur the lines. I see a three-way war on morals happening today and it's being pressed on kids at an early age. The characters are self-esteem, effort, and performance.

The self-esteem advocates want everybody to feel good. But how can you do that in a performance-based world as they get older? Is a science fair going to give out two first-place medals? If one student made the baking soda volcano and another student created a solar-powered, no-emission cargo truck that will change transportation in our country, I doubt they both get a blue ribbon. It's very important to develop self-esteem and I strongly believe in that. We can send that message and develop those self-esteem traits in noncompetitive performance environments. But the fact is, we need to prepare our young people for performing and self-esteem by itself won't get them a paycheck one day. Sooner or later, they are going to be properly assessed and it won't feel good so we might as well help them now.

Do you know who Maurice Ralph Hilleman was? Most are not familiar with that name but should be. He was a microbiologist. Not just any microbiologist either. He is responsible for saving millions of lives every year. Maurice

Hilleman developed vaccines for the measles, mumps, hepatitis A and B, chickenpox, meningitis, pneumonia, and *Haemophilus influenzae* (the strain that caused the 1892 influence pandemic). Finding a vaccine for any one of those would have been a lifetime achievement. But developing vaccines for eight different health ailments is unfathomable.

You likely haven't heard of him because he is very humble. Most microbiologists name their vaccines after themselves. Hilleman did not name a single vaccine after himself. He wanted to heal and serve others. When he made his first trial of the hepatitis B vaccine, he injected himself first to prove to the world it was safe.

Here is a story that I am sure we can all relate to. Hilleman predicted that a strain of flu in Hong Kong was unlike anything we had seen in the US and could be catastrophic if it came here. After reading an article on 17 April 1957 in the *New York Times* regarding the situation in Hong Kong, he said, "My God. This is the pandemic. It's here!" It became known as the Asian Flu and would kill 1.1 million people.

Thanks to Hilleman, 40 million doses of the vaccine were created before it hit American soil. 110,000 Americans lost their lives, but according to US Surgeon General Leonard Burney, the virus would have infected millions had there not been a vaccine.

Maurice Hilleman saved millions of lives then and now with his vaccines, but do you know what his driving force was? He had a "rent's due" moment. His "want to" became his "got to" in March 1963. His five-year-old daughter came into his room late one night, ill with swollen glands and a sore throat. She had contracted the mumps, which was a potentially fatal illness. With no cure at the time, Hilleman went to work and successfully created a vaccine which is still used to save lives today.

Maurice Hilleman was a true hero with a "rent's due" mentality.

If you and I are able to change perceptions of our tasks and hit them violently head on, our worth is limitless. In our classrooms, we can use that. I love to share stories like Hilleman's to influence student perception. One remarkable thing about being a teacher is that you have the amazing power to influence minds and processes if you are able to get out in front of the perpetrators that harm their thinking.

It's incredible to think that I have the power to propel students or enable them, to make them feel like they can do it or let them know that they cannot. I can remove the roadblocks that stop them or place more traffic in their path. I can humanize or dehumanize them to create mindsets. What other job is this powerful?

One of the best examples of a "rent's due" attitude often occurs when someone is stricken with cancer. Cancer is a scary word and chances are that you know someone who has had or is currently having this fight. It's a nasty illness that tries to destroy hope and can even take dignity and happiness. If we don't have it, we could. The day that any patient gets this diagnosis is a day they will never, ever forget.

This is a true "rent's due" moment, and cancer is an "all in" fight. You and I are not able to cure cancer. We are not able to send it into remission either. But I'll tell you what we *can* do. We can help the patient fight. We can rally in numbers around this brave soul and help them compete to win each day. We can help them have a "rent's due" mindset because quitting is not an option.

We can spend time with them so the voices in their heads are quiet just for the time you are with them. We can drive them to treatments and appointments to share that moment with them so they are not alone. We can send them constant encouragement in the way of emails, texts, and handwritten notes. We can send them keepsakes with meaning like a cross for them to have in their pocket, a special photo from a perfect day or an amazing quote that, at least for one day, inspires hope. Lastly, we can grow from their bravery and experience in this situation.

Fairly recently my mother, who was always as healthy and as tough as any person I've ever met, asked me if I would take her to a doctor because her leg was hurting. I can count on one hand how many times in my life my mom went to a doctor, so I knew this had to be tremendously painful for her. My brother and I were there when the doctor confirmed that it was cancer. It was a day that none of us would forget. The rent had just become due.

Our family was "all in" and it required all hands on deck. My brother is very successful in the business world and I say that not to brag but with tremendous pride in all that he has accomplished and the integrity that he has done it with. The business world can be a "dog eat dog" environment, as well as one where money and success change people. That never happened to him because he is the mentally toughest person I've ever known. It seems like no matter the circumstance he is always in control of his thoughts. He's still happily married to his ninth grade girlfriend, often drives a car that isn't as nice as the ones the high school kids I teach drive, and never talks about success or money.

My brother and I met after the doctor left the room. We made a plan of action and our "rent's due" mindsets took over. We had a plan for getting our mother to and from every treatment, keeping hope, and winning the battles that would naturally occur in her head.

The bad news was that the cancer had spread to a size of a volleyball in her leg and it was aggressive. The good news was that her veteran doctor told us that she had qualified for a new and promising immunotherapy that was valued somewhere near a million dollars for treatment and both her and her insurance were qualified to get it. That really gave her hope as we walked out of that hospital.

A little later we were asked to come back to Baltimore for a meeting. My brother and I were in the room with our mother when the veteran doctor walked in. He told my mother that she had a low iron count and because of that, she was now disqualified for the treatment. He explained that the situation had now changed and that the outcome was now not good. Then he walked out of the room. The whole meeting probably took two minutes. In two minutes, the damage had been done and her hope and mindset had been destroyed. The rent was no due a little earlier.

Things would get worse. The cancer spread and put so much stress on her femur that the only option left was to remove her leg. My father served our country as a career for most of his life. My mom grew up in a coal-mining town and then traveled the globe with him, maybe that's where she learned to be an absolute fighter. But even with her demeanor and the mental tactics used from my brother and I, cancer was getting the best of her. I could feel that she was losing her will to fight and it was killing me.

Then entered two "rent's due" game-changers. The first was Dr. Vincent Ng. Dr. Ng performed the thirteenth-hour surgery to remove her leg. He would become and remain one of the greatest heroes in our family's lives. Not just because of his incredible skill as a doctor but as a caring human being. He would drive across the city at all hours of the night, including on Easter to encourage her in person.

Even when it was not his job to do that, he would leave his home and his family on his own time to do that. One doctor coldly broke her will to live and another warmly restored it.

The second game-changer came when my mother was at her rock bottom. Her leg had been removed and she was lying in a hospital bed in the shock trauma unit where she would stay for months. Things were really tough.

Every day an amazing woman named Delores would walk into her room to change her wastebasket. I would see her walk in and hear her say, "Hello Phyllis! You look beautiful today. Pretty soon you will be out on your front porch sipping lemonade watching your grandchildren play. Can't you just see it, Phyllis?"

My mom would light up like a Christmas tree. I could see her hope restoring right before my eyes. This wonderful woman decided to make her job description not be a job restriction. She joined the "rent's due" crusade and absolutely restored hope with kindness and visualization. It was incredible. What Delores taught me was that WE ALL HAVE POWER to change a mindset and that is when amazing things start to happen. My mom would start working out five to ten times a day on her own, right there in that hospital bed using surgical tubing as resistance bands. Her health metric numbers became amazing and today she walks at least a mile a day up and down her driveway on a prosthetic leg.

I learned a lot of valuable lessons through this experience. You and I have power. You and I can make a difference with our attitudes, influences, and mindsets. When things look tough, you and I can pay the rent if our mindset is right. Attack today like your rent is due.

9

HIGH-PERFORMANCE LEARNING

"If you are not willing to learn, no one can help you. If you are determined to learn, no one can stop you."

— Zig Ziglar

Years of trying to get students and athletes performing at a high level have taught me a few tricks in getting the minds of others to a high-performing level under stress. How can we as educators and they as students handle the emotions and detractors to performance? Assessing is supposed to be about measuring what they know and what they can do. But I don't always see it that way. If I put your desk in the middle lane of a busy freeway at rush hour, I doubt that your score on any test would be as good as it would have been in an environment that you are comfortable with.

The fact is, there are obstacles to performing. There always has been and likely, there always will be. As a baseball coach, if I am working with a pitcher in a bullpen during a practice, that young man might perform well. Maybe he throws mostly strikes with great velocity and movement. But when he is pitching live in a game that counts, he struggles. What happened? His performance was impacted by any number of factors. I assessed him to be proficient at a skill, but the environment impacted his state of performance and that means that I didn't really prepare him well. High-performance learning occurs when a variety of factors have actually been addressed and serviced.

In that example, the failure by that pitcher was all mine. I did not realistically prepare him. My preparation was having him throw in a bullpen to a catcher. That's it. But when he pitched in the real game, he had his mother and girlfriend looking at him. He had opposing fans booing him and rooting for his failure. He had another human being standing in that batter's box trying to compete on every pitch against him. And he had an umpire assessing each and every pitch he threw. I didn't prepare him for any of that, I just tried to improve his skill. His failure was my failure. We do this in teaching daily where we focus on an assessment without accounting for dozens of external factors.

I want to listen to students as much as I talk to them, to get an understanding of the feelings they have when I try to teach them. Anxiety and pressure are real inhibitors that creep into education easily and often. For example, I never use the term "deadline." It's just a negative, anxiety-provoking term. I want students to be excited to turn a project in and have some pride in that. Do you know where the term "deadline" came from? Lacking proper materials during the Civil War, prisoners would have lines drawn around them in the dirt. If they crossed the line, they were shot by the guard to enforce the rule to others.

Just Breathe

Try this for a second, close your eyes. Take a big, deep breath. I'm talking about a five-second breath. Inhale through your nose only. As you are inhaling, simultaneously think about a stressor that's bothering you. Think about it as a dark cloud in the room. As you are breathing in, picture that cloud being completely sucked up into you like you're a vacuum cleaner. Hold it for six seconds and then exhale slowly for five more. When you exhale, picture that entire dark cloud leaving you and going into an airtight vault, never to be opened again. When you are done exhaling, open your eyes and see that vault slamming shut forever. This signifies that you just dealt with that stressor and now you're done with it. Boom! Forward with focus from here.

I'm a believer that tactics like this work for positive performance. Essentially, you are combining the mental and the physical for one big stress-relieving, high-performing, sixteen-second action that can pay big dividends. If we are going to do our best for students, we ourselves should be using tactics like this. It's having a contingency plan for when a situation or environment grows stressful. Stressors are never going to stop coming at you. So let's address them and let's prepare for them.

You have probably heard people say "take a deep breath" a hundred times. People have been using breathing tactics for years to increase performance. In our teaching world, we can use this to impact student behavior. Think about the student who is filled with the sudden emotions of rage or pain. Breathing techniques can be used to calm them down and get them back to neutral. We can also use breathing techniques in areas of academics, athletics, band, performing arts, clubs, or some other activity where the idea of performing can cause anxiety. These strategies can certainly be used for teachers, coaches, and administrators as well, to get us into our high-performing zones.

So what's really going on there? Do you mean to tell me that how I breathe makes a difference in my ability to function at my highest level as a teacher, coach, or administrator? Well, yes actually. Scientifically, the act of taking deep breaths is called "diaphragmatic breathing." That's a fancy way to say that deep breathing actually does some pretty good things to your body that you can use for high performance. Your diaphragm is actually a sheet of muscle in between your chest and abdomen. When you breathe in, your diaphragm moves downward, pulling your lungs with it, and presses against your abdominal organs. As you breathe out, the diaphragm pushes back and expels the carbon dioxide. At the bottom of the lungs are many important blood vessels that are vital for carrying rich oxygen to the body.

When we have shallow breathing, we shorten the diaphragm's range of motion and it never gets to those bottom vessels. This can make you short of breath and cause anxiety throughout the body. Deep breathing leads the diaphragm to pull full levels of oxygen in and activates those lower vessels in your lungs. This actually decreases your heart rate and lowers your blood pressure.

Guess what type of breathing dominates performance situations? You got it, short and rapid breathing and usually through the mouth. It's an involuntary response to life's stressful moments. That student taking the test, that athlete during the game, that performer during their show, and even that teacher, administrator, or coach before their big speech...all become low-performance breathers. So if you want to make an easy improvement to increase performance and decrease anxiety, be mindful of your breathing.

The Brain

Here is a useful fact for teaching high-performance learning. The brain's active short-term memory lasts for about twenty to thirty seconds. That's it. Most brains hold numbers in their short-term memory for about seven seconds on average and letters for nine seconds. Consider short-term memory like a spill of water on warm concrete that is evaporating fast. If you want to drive home a point, you might need to be repetitive in an effort to get it to literally soak in. Revisiting lessons and points that were made earlier as a warm-up the following day is a good practice for retention.

I've always felt strongly that the first week of every class, in every subject, should be dedicated to just two things: developing relationships and figuring out how each student learns.

It's inconceivable to me to even think about teaching students any material until I know the students and they know me. I promise to teach them all the same when they promise to all learn the same. Science tells me that each brain has different capabilities and disabilities.

Everything I've read on the brain says that multitasking involving attention spans is actually impossible to our human brains. We can go back and forth between tasks but we can't actually do them both at the same time. Research says that not only does multitasking actually make both tasks take longer but our error rate goes up by an average of 50 percent when we multitask.

When I think about my educational experience as a student, I think about the difficulty that I had focusing. Multitasking was part of my daily routine. I didn't realize how I learned. There were countless distractions both around me and in my own head. I either dealt with the distractions poorly or I didn't deal with them at all.

Looking back, each of those distractions turned into me multitasking. My brain would shift its focus from reading or writing to whatever distraction my eyes caught. It could have been another student running their paper to the teacher, a question someone else asked, or my eyes wandering to the other problems ahead. I created a multitasking environment in my head.

Today, I try to relate the distractions that I felt to what students might feel. Distractions allow for multitasking and multitasking leads to higher error rates. Knowing how you learn can be an amazing weapon against this. Strategies and tactics to reduce the mind's ability to wander can have significant results. Too much silence, not enough silence, vision, and even energy levels can impact a particular student's ability to multitask and lose focus.

Remember that story about Goldilocks the three bears? Too hot, too cold, and just right were the assessments. I think that learning atmospheres are a lot like that. For me, silence was deadly. The voices in my mind were never as loud as when the room was completely silent. I just couldn't learn like that. A little background noise seemed to quiet my brain and allow me to focus. Too much background noise and I became distracted again. I love this well-worded poem written by Ms. Moem related to the voice we sometimes hear:

> Do you hear that voice? That little voice?
> The one inside your head.
> You make a choice and that little voice
> says "No, you can't" instead.
> So silence that voice, that little voice,

and show it who is boss.
Don't let that voice, that little voice,
Be the master of opportunities lost.

Some might prefer a quiet environment and see any type of noise as a distraction. Did you know that the Microsoft headquarters in Redmond, Washington, has the quietest room on earth? Sound measures twenty decibels below the threshold of human hearing. While I value some noise, others value a quiet atmosphere for high performance. Well guess what? The "real world" works like that too. When our students enter the workforce there are jobs with both quiet and busy atmospheres.

How Do They Learn?

Focusing on how people learn and perform are not exclusive thoughts to education. Some businesses are smart enough to value the environments that their employees learn and perform highly in. Google has become recognized as one of the leaders in valuing these high-performing atmospheres. Google recognized studies showing a workplace that encourages collaborative learning increases productivity by 15 percent.

They believe in shaping their environment in a variety of ways to encourage high performance. One such way is their 150-foot rule. At their New York headquarters, no part of their office is ever more than 150 feet away from food. They built coffee lounges, cafeterias, and even a restaurant to encourage employees to hang out in areas socially while eating to collaborate. Yes, even eating is collaborative and productive there. At some of their other locations they have office putting greens, beach volleyball, climbing walls, and even a jungle, all built with the idea that the environment will encourage socializing and socializing will encourage collaboration.

Acknowledging that not every learner performs high in that type of environment, some businesses choose the opposite theme. Many companies have created quiet think tanks, meditative zones, and old=school library spaces so that their employees can center and be one with their thoughts. Energy pods that are basically comfortable lounge chairs with hoods and covers have become incredibly popular and even allow rest for employees to restore themselves with catnaps. Seems like a smart concept to build environments that allow people to get into their high-performing zones. Let's do that for you and your students!

Another issue that I had in my learning and performing at times was my wandering eyes. My peripheral vision was very active. In some cases that was helpful but particularly with reading...it was not. My eyes could be reading the text and somehow they still had the ability to see any classmate moving. My eyes could also be reading the text while skimming words and sentences ahead causing me to have no clue what I was reading in real time.

Years later, when I noticed my students were having the same problem, a fantastic colleague shared with me the most impactful piece of reading equipment that I have ever used. An index card that cost about two cents. That's right, putting the edge of that card on the line that students were reading blocked out the coming text and changed reading speeds and retention right before my eyes. It took seconds. No long training of the brain is needed. Just hand the student a simple index card and watch the magic work.

Olympic gold medalist sensation Simone Biles has always been a champion that young gymnasts everywhere look up to. In 2016, she became a champion to kids in education as well. Hackers published her confidential medical files revealing that she had ADHD and took medication for it. Her bold and fast public response was that having ADHD was nothing to be ashamed of. She went so far as to say that ADHD can be a superpower. She became and continues to be an advocate and champion for kids everywhere with learning disabilities.

Reducing distractions is both individual and specific. What works for one student may be the polar opposite to what works for another. Can you manipulate each particular student's environment within the same class? If you can, you really have something special! Reduce the student's ability to multitask and you can watch them change before your eyes. If a student is floundering in his or her current environs, maybe it's time to try something different.

I used to fight cell phones in class every day, and honestly, I'm not sure I always won that battle. Did you know that Facebook has more users than the population of the United States, China, and Brazil combined? It has well over two billion active users. If kids can learn to type and communicate on Facebook, then they can type and communicate in my class. They are learning differently today than when we were in school. We have to account for that. Ask students to speak up and answer a question and you might hear crickets. Ask them to take out their phones and text their opinion and you will get plenty of communication going.

Young people love technology and anything they can see on a screen they have learned to interact with. It's a powerful way to make an impact on young people. Did you know that when Disney released the movie *The Princess and the Frog*, that more than fifty children were hospitalized with salmonella from kissing frogs? That's impactful. If young people are into something, they connect and learn from it. Maybe we are not asking the right questions with education. Maybe we should be asking, "What are they into and how can we use it to instruct?" Video games and TikToks are all the rage right now, what if we could tap into that somehow? Instead of fighting it, maybe we spin it and go with it. What creative ways can you think of to use today's trends to connect our young people with high-performing learning?

Communication

I think there should be a class offered to educators on communication. I'm serious, I think that it is that important and a true trait of high performers. This could stop a lot of things that go wrong in our profession and really benefit students. When I see or hear a person with great communication skills, I try to pay attention and steal what I can to grow.

I see communication as a simple three-part process. You have a message, a sender, and a receiver. It's amazing how many times that can go wrong! Countries have literally gone to war with each other over this breakdown. The substance of a message can be good or bad. As much as we would like it to be, communication won't always be positive. Sometimes the message has to be direct, reprimanding, or negative. We can deliver negative messages with good communication. With that said, how you send it and how you receive it are things we can improve.

When most people hear the term "communication," they immediately think talking. We forget that this is only 50 percent of the equation. Rarely do people value listening or practice the skills associated with listening as much as we do sending the message, but it is critical to being an effective teacher.

Have you ever done a lesson with students on listening? I believe that at the start of a school year, every student (and staff member) should have a lesson on how to listen, followed by how to verbally communicate. If you want to be a good communicator, the very first step is to become a good listener. One type of listening is referred to as active listening.

Being active in your listening will do two really amazing things. First, it will allow the person you are communicating with to understand that you are interested in them. It's personal, it's attentive, and it's being present. You can be right in front of someone while they are speaking but not be present. That is not a relation-enhancing trait with students or colleagues.

Ways to Actively Listen

- Do not interrupt. This makes others feel undervalue and that you have little respect for them.
- When finished, repeat to the person what they just said. It will help for clarity and retention.
- When they finish, you can communicate what you just heard in your own words. "So, what I just took from that was…"
- Make sure your eyes, posture, and facial expressions explain that you are attentive and listening. Make your body say, "I'm giving you my undivided attention and you matter."
- When possible, try not to immediately counter or outdo their point when they finish speaking. It's not a contest.

The second thing that actively listening will do is allow you to avoid misinterpreting the message and retain more information. Yes, it can be a memory enhancer! We teach thousands of students in our careers and we are responsible for remembering each and every one of their names when you see them around town. So when a student tells me their name, I try to always actively listen.

When I ask a student their name they might say, "It's Johnny." As I shake their hand (another aspect of actively listening), I might say, "Johnny. Okay, Johnny, where are you from?" He might reply, "Frederick." To which I would actively reply, "Johnny from Frederick. Well Johnny from Frederick, it is a pleasure to meet you." In that quick exchange I just communicated to him that he was more than just a name to me. I communicated that I was present with him and giving him some undivided attention. I communicated that I was interested in meeting him. And by hearing his name not once, but four times during the exchange, I increased the odds of somebody as slow as me retaining his name.

Being a skilled verbal communicator is a challenge as well. Maybe you are a good listener but feel like you always put your foot in your mouth. Being great at verbally communicating can change mere sentences into useful power. Power to motivate, inspire, and let the receiver know that you care, with intangibles other than the message. If you are poor at it, even the best messages could have no meaning, offend, or disengage learners or colleagues. Try eliminating any bad verbal habits.

Negative Communicators to Avoid

- Avoid using words like "You" and "Your." Before you finish those sentences, you just put the receiver into defense mode. "I" statements are much more effective.
- Avoid novocaine-like qualifiers. Saying phrases like "no offense" or "don't take this personally but" are negative communicators before the message is even sent.
- Avoid talking about yourself once they finish. Saying, "I know all about that" or "You don't have to tell me..." are verbal ways to minimize the other person's communication and value.
- Avoid using verbal "time buyers" like "umm," "and," and "like." It can weaken a good message and give the appearance of uncertainty.
- Avoid rambling and land your plane. Be clear and be concise. Communicate the message. Belabor a point and you weaken your point.

If excellence is doing all of the little things right, do we actually spend time planning or practicing communication? I know that I have overlooked this often. If communication is critical to success, we should value practicing it as educators. Do you know when communication becomes the most difficult? When it has to be a tough conversation. Whether it has to be had with a student, a colleague, or an administrator, tough conversations are not fun and require skill.

There are two ways to have a tough conversation: planned and unplanned. When you know the problem isn't going away, you either deal with the issue or it will deal with you. Often, it's not something we are looking forward to, so it gets postponed. The next time you have an issue looming, consider the battleground. Would you rather have a say in the environment and audience or leave it to chance?

Unplanned communication can be volatile and ineffective. This communication can have an unintended audience and that audience can have an influence on behaviors. I've seen many times where the communication wasn't about sending and receiving messages, it was about saving face or playing to an audience. Often members of the audience will add their approval or disapproval and suddenly it's not a two-way conversation. Avoid this with planning.

Benefits of Planned Tough Conversations

- You can choose a warm or neutral location.
- You can control the audience in attendance.
- You can plan the itinerary of the conversation.
- You are addressing a stressor in your life in a timely manner.
- You can establish rules and boundary lines for effectiveness and respect throughout the meeting.

Planned conversations to tough problems may still be uncomfortable but at least you can control the environment and the platform. You can have the conversation in a place conducive to productive talking with as many stressors removed from the situation as possible. You can also plan your conversation itinerary carefully and keep an element of respect. If it's a really tough conversation, don't be afraid to set meeting guidelines that ensure the respectful environment is kept regardless of viewpoints. Shouting, name-calling, and insults will overshadow messages during a conversation, and you might be better off ending the meeting promptly, as opposed to pushing through. Band-aids don't fix bullet holes, so end a conversation when you feel the line of respect has been destroyed. Being proactive with tough conversations may help you solve some tough problems in your career and personal life.

I have a lot of respect for the teachers who value learning processes as much as educational skills. The fact is, we are not all born smart or talented, but we can find a way to figure ourselves out and get to our own high-performance level. This old Native American parable sums up how we should be tackling high-performance learning.

A Cherokee Elder was teaching his grandson about life. "A fight is going on inside me," he said to the boy. "It is a terrible fight and it is between two wolves. One wolf is evil—he is anger, envy, sorrow, regret, greed, arrogance, self-pity, guilt, resentment, inferiority, lies, false pride, superiority, and ego."

He continued, "The other wolf is good—he is joy, peace, love, hope, serenity, humility, kindness, benevolence, empathy, generosity, truth, compassion, and faith. The same fight is going on inside you—and inside every other person, too."

The grandson thought about it for a minute and then asked his grandfather, "Which wolf will win?" The old Cherokee simply replied, "The one you feed."

Let's feed our teachers and students positivity. Let's feed educators professional developments that connect them and build relationships with students. Let's feed students strategies and tactics specific to the way that they learn. Let's make education a passionate and positive feeling for teachers again. Let's go!

10

A HEALTHY YOU

"The problem with doing nothing is not knowing when you're finished."

— Benjamin Franklin

As I watched the debate during Covid unfold over when to send teachers back into schools, it became clear to me that many just didn't understand what teachers do. It seemed to me that there was a strong disconnect between opinion and reality of a teacher's demands and some of that was coming from governors and local elected officials. You battle every day to get up early, stay late, and make a dent in that huge to-do list that each day brings. Sometimes it feels like you are running as hard as you can but when you look up, you haven't moved forward. This is still the greatest job in the world but...it comes with a warning label. Be careful not to neglect your health.

Let's face it, teaching has some unhealthy aspects to it. Tight timelines, demanding parents, and an ever growing job description can cause you serious stress. Let's focus on something that has nothing to do with teaching but has everything to do with teaching. Let's focus on getting and keeping you healthy.

Sitting has been identified as the new smoking. Being sedentary and sitting around destroys the body from the inside out and increases our chances for numerous diseases and illnesses. High blood pressure, back problems, depression, slow metabolism, and weight gain are just the tip of the iceberg. So for physical health, we have to move. That's it! There's no secret exercise, just move.

The Greatest Medication

You can actually help yourself while you are teaching. Standing up, getting steps in by pacing back and forth as you are lecturing, and leading stretch-based brain breaks are things you can do right there in your classroom. I love walking to students when they have a question or pacing the room for proximity behavior control because it helps me stay active. And if you must sit, tap your foot constantly for better blood circulation. Wear a cheap step counter you might be surprised how many miles you can move in the course of a school day. Plus, this will get your oxygen flowing, avoiding that mid-day energy dip. You're going to need all the energy you can get.

Getting the body moving is medicine for the brain as well. Did you know that although your body stops growing in your teens, the human brain actually grows in size until your late 40s? It actually shrinks after that but is not less effective. The brain uses more of your body's energy than any other organ. Twenty percent of all of your body's energy is used by your brain. So when we tell students to work out their brains or we call assignments exercises, we are not wrong.

The Dent Neurologic Institute says this about exercise for the brain:

"It has been noted that exercise promotes the production of neurotrophins, leading to greater brain plasticity, resulting in better memory and learning. In addition to neurotrophins, exercise also results in an increase of neurotransmitters in the brain, specifically serotonin and norepinephrine which boost information, processing and mood."

So the next question is, "How can we use that in schools?" I am a firm believer that physical education and movement in schools is a vital piece of development for minds young and old alike.

Dr. Robert Butler from the National Institute of Aging says, "If you could bottle it or put it into a pill, exercise would be the most widely prescribed and beneficial medication in the world." Something this impactful to learning and health should not be ignored. Imagine building it into the school day periodically. I love hearing stories of schools that are building physical activity into their everyday routines for teachers and students.

Ways to Build Exercise into the School Day

- No shortcuts. Take the long way to everything, hit the stairs, and forget using the school phone when you can walk and deliver a message.
- Move within your room. Stand, erase, write, talk with your hands, pace the room...Just keep moving!
- Take brain breaks after students have been sitting for twenty minutes. Build in big moving exercises where height level changes. Do body squats, use

chairs to perform sit-down-and-get-ups, do touch-the-floor-touch-the-sky moves, and so on.
- Play music in between classes encouraging students to move and groove. This will also boost moods so it's a win-win.
- Instead of placing materials near each other, design a route that makes them move. It's like a scavenger hunt with a step counter.

Your health reformation starts with changing your views about getting to a destination. Have you ever seen two people get into a heated argument over the farthest parking spot away from a store? I haven't. Change the way you look at things. Our psychology has a lot to do with how successful we are with our health and fitness.

It is so easy to be negative or quit. So address your past experiences and understand that they have absolutely nothing to do with today. The only connection to your past is you not having amnesia. Try this, instead of focusing on the negative, focus positively. Don't say "I'm not going to sit around" or "I'm not eating this and that," instead focus on what you will do and what you will eat. Positive focuses like, "I'm going to exercise for 100 straight days" or "I'm going to drink six bottles of water every day." Make your focus be the great habits you are adding. That enforces you being the "New You" instead of trying not to be the person who has failed before.

Here's another psychological trick for your health. Use visual enforcers daily to keep your long-term goals fresh and in sight. If I'm trying to lose five pounds, I place two jars on my sink in the bathroom. One jar is filled with five of something to represent five pounds. Five rocks, five coins, or when I'm really serious, five twenty-dollar bills.

Every day I weigh myself and if I lost a pound, I take one of the items from the start jar and place it into the goal jar. Moving one of those twenties from one jar to the other feels pretty darn good and it motivates me to keep climbing closer to my goals. But if the scale said I have to take a hard-earned bill out of the goal jar and put it back in the starting jar...that really, really stings.

I have found this to be a great way to hold myself accountable. You would be surprised how many times I thought about that bathroom jar as someone offered me dessert. When you accomplish your goal and successfully move that last item into that goal jar, reward yourself and do something with that money that makes you feel good.

Most brains are preprogrammed to take shortcuts, easy routes, and close parking spots. Spin that! Let's get our teachers and young people looking at movement as a privilege. Add fun obstacles or enhancements in the halls that promote exercise. Some schools have slides inside their buildings that are accessible by taking the steps. Having everchanging artwork, motivational quotes, or outstanding schoolwork on the hallway walls weekly could pique student interest enough to get them moving to see it. This would also be a great way to enhance school culture.

Speaking of school culture, use your creativity to get students moving related to your culture. Maybe in your building a three-minute trendy rehearsed dance to a popular song would get them going. How can you lure your young people into accidentally raising their heart rates between classes?

A great way to help staff engage in activity is to do it in large numbers. By getting a group together, you may have better results. This can offer both a warm social element of support as well as accountability. Years of training people has taught me that the mind will quit and let yourself down but when there is someone else involved, quitting becomes harder. You will let yourself down more often than you will let others down. Having partners and fun groups will help you get through those days when you just aren't feeling it. So will the idea of having a bigger cause. Running for yourself is one thing, but doing it for a heartfelt mission or charity will give you that fire that you are looking for.

Consider starting a club, before or after school. A run bunch, lifting group, yoga class, or whatever other fun exercise trend you feel can take off with those you know. Log your hours or miles and see if you can get to a mighty number as your goal. Or just ask someone in your building to walk with you in hopes of helping them get started. It's a great way to build relationships too. You move, they move, next you have a healthy school.

Addition by Subtraction

The nature of our career empowers us to serve others, and that is a great thing. But if you are anything like me, you sometimes get yourself into more opportunities with good intentions, than you have time to do. The problem is that something has to be sacrificed and often, it's your quality of life. I'm horrendous with this. I'll get so incredibly busy and stressed with timelines and then complain that I have too much going on. It's nobody else's fault but mine. That two-letter word is a powerful one and sometimes you have to learn how and when to use it. It's natural to not want to let someone down, but if you don't advocate for yourself, who will?

Satchel Paige said, "How old would you be if you didn't know how old you are?" Do you remember being a really young kid without a care in the world? No bills to pay, no lengthy lists of things to get done, just wondering what someone else was making you for dinner that night? Our minds get convoluted and polluted from all of the stuff that we take on. Instead of doing one thing well, I'll do twenty things mediocre or poorly with a stress level that's not healthy.

Try addition by subtraction. Focus on decluttering your life. We all make new resolutions and goals yearly, but do we ever sit down and brainstorm how we can declutter our lives? What can you take off your plate that would help restore you to a healthy level? Imagine having only one target on your to-do list today. I bet that you would do it well. When our attention is in too many places, it weakens us and makes us average at what we do. So start simplifying your life for a better performance and a better peace of mind.

Stress could be the most serious threat to an educator's health. Stressors come in a degree of levels. You have your green level (raised heartbeat and anxiety), your yellow level (headache, ulcer, and chest pains) and then your red level (the freak-out or get-to-a-doctor stage). And what one may deem not too stressful another could see as catastrophic. Stress perceived is stress, and it can do serious damage.

I once heard a story that took place in a section of Los Angeles common to shootings in the nineties. An elderly woman lived in a tough neighborhood where crime and drive-by shootings were common. The elderly woman went to the grocery store to pick up a few things on a hot summer day. On her way home, she got the idea to make a quick stop at the beauty salon while leaving her groceries in her car. One of the grocery items was a pressurized canister of premade biscuits.

The temperature inside the car became very warm while she was in that beauty salon. When she was finished and driving home, she heard a loud bang and felt something hit the back of her head. When she reached around to feel what it was, she felt what in reality was a wad of the biscuit dough, which had exploded from the heat. Sadly, she thought she had been shot in the head and went into shock.

Was there anything physically wrong with her? No, but high amounts of perceived stress and anxiety are still harmful. And they still do the same amount of damage. So when a fellow teacher or young person has tremendous anxiety over anything at all, we have to take it seriously.

Teaching is stressful, and I want you to have an army of weapons at your disposal to combat this stress. I love using these tactics for my students and I believe they can help us too. You can use four different senses to help you. I believe you can use sight, sound, smell, and feel as weapons against stress for you and your students.

Sight

What are you putting your eyes on? There is never a shortage of drama, despair, or conflict to look at in our world. We can stop taking what is fed to us and create our own images. I want visions that destress me all around my line of sight. It's like building defense weapons around my castle for the time when the attacks come.

We know that calming visions produce dopamine and serotonin in our brains, which can lower our cortisol levels caused by stress. Walk into a relaxation spa and you are sure to see pictures on the walls for that exact purpose. Doctors will recommend vacations to stressed individuals with high and unhealthy vital numbers because doing so can free the mind from work routines while the aesthetics calm the brain. You can have beautiful, relaxing, vacation-like images all around you whether it is in your home, your office, as a screensaver or in your classroom.

For your personal health, try placing eye candy at home too. Fish tanks are known to be extremely soothing. Today, you don't even have to buy a real one. You can avoid the work by making your television into your very own fish tank. Cable networks often have free channels for this, or you can simply go to YouTube. In seconds, you have your very own stress-reducing moving art.

Another fantastic way to use your eyes to destress is watching a flickering fire. An indoor or outdoor fireplace, a fire ring, or a bonfire on a Friday night might just be your ticket after a long and hard week of teaching. There is something about relaxing by a fire that will help declutter your mind and get you back to neutral for next week. It's not nearly the same, but in a pinch, you can turn your television or device into a fireplace as well with crackling sounds and warm images using the same platforms as the fish tanks.

Sound

According to a 2018 report by the National Center for Biotechnology Information, "Some studies have shown the mere act of listening to natural sounds is capable of inducing a state of relaxation via stress-relieving effects within the endocrine and autonomic nervous systems." Listening to natural noises like water, wind, birds, and rain is medicine for your mind. You can install an inexpensive water fountain in your home in minutes or use technology to listen to nature radio in your home, car, or on a planning period.

Aside from natural sounds, music has long been known to have an impact on our brains and can be used by educators to destress. In a 2006 press release, researchers at Stanford University said, "Listening to music seems to be able to change brain functioning to the same extent as medication." German philosopher Emanuel Kant called music "the quickening art." In some studies, music has shown a connection of neural pathways and has restored lost functions. Create playlists that you can use as your Advil for those tough days.

Another tactic is to hear...nothing. How often do we actually declutter our mind with silence? Using silence or perhaps some Zenlike music for meditating has been shown to actually reset you.

I remember hearing a story about a grandmother who watched ten children during the day by herself. She cooked, cleaned, educated all day, every day. But for ten minutes after lunch each and every day, that was her untouchable time. She sat in a rocking chair with her eyes closed, humming a hymn in complete solitude. The children knew that was not a time they could approach her. For her sanity and longevity, she built that ten minutes stubbornly into her day and it worked for her. Maybe this could work for you?

Smell

What you smell can have an impact on how you feel. It's called aromatherapy. Smelling rosemary or cinnamon can help fight physical exhaustion, headaches, and mental fatigue. The scent of peppermint is an energy booster and can improve thinking while reducing brain fog. But the aromas we need for stress reduction are lemon, lavender, and jasmine. Lavender in particular helps relieve nervous tension and depression.

You can build this into your preemptive strike on stress with diffusers, oils, candles, or air fresheners. What you inhale quickly goes to your brain, so let's use that for our health.

Feel

What you touch or what touches you can reduce stress and be used as medicine. Pets have been shown as effective tools to use against stress and depression. Programs exist for those with special needs to access horses as therapy. Riding or petting horses often has miraculous impacts on nervous systems and produces serotonin.

Dogs and cats are being used to bring happiness and decrease cortisol to those with trauma. From war veterans with PTSD to children in long-term care hospitals, pets are doing wonderful things. There are programs for those who are incarcerated to spend time holding a dog or a cat, which is having scientific results to humanize and restore emotions. Petting, holding, or being licked by a loving animal can be your daily medicine.

If I asked you to quickly name somebody who is a great picture of health, who immediately comes to mind? Chances are that you just thought of somebody with six pack abs, drinking a green smoothie while wearing a Speedo. Often, when we hear the word "health," we automatically think of physical health. Television is loaded with physically fit young people spending their parents' millions on reality shows, surrounded by a sea of dysfunction and mental health issues. I'd say they are fit but not healthy. We also equate health to good nutrition.

Perhaps your picture of health was a vegan. But I doubt that anybody just named a great sleeper.

You feeling healthy is paramount to you being a great teacher. We value exercise and nutrition but most of us do not hold sleep in the same standing. Are you aware that the periodic table, the understanding of the structure of DNA, and even Google were ideas that were formed during sleep? More and more studies are being released related to the impact of sleep on our bodies and the results are astounding. Quality sleep is essential for your brain function, mood, and energy levels which happen to be three of the most important things teachers need to bring to work every day to be effective.

Your brain stays active while you sleep by removing toxins that build up during your day. Ever wonder why your body yawns when it is tired? Research suggests that yawning cools the brain. Our brains actually increase in temperature when deprived of sleep. Much like diet and exercise allows our heart to function properly, sleep does that for our brains. The Mayo Clinic claims that adults need seven to nine hours of sleep. Our high school students should have eight to ten hours and our elementary and middle school students should have nine to eleven.

Unlike diet and exercise, focusing on your sleep pays immediate dividends. We log and analyze our food consumption and exercise performed, but I doubt most track their sleep. There are great apps that can really help you with this. Search your app store if interested in the latest type. Common things that destroy our sleep are blue light, a racing mind, and chemicals from eating late at night. Here are some tactics for a better night's sleep so you can wake up tomorrow and be a game-changer to kids!

Take Your Nights Back Tactics

- Block blue light, especially at night. Get a pair of blue light–blocking glasses or an app for your smartphone or computer that blocks it for you.
- Take a magnesium, melatonin, or lavender supplement to give yourself a better quality of sleep and to fall asleep faster.
- Get a sleep app to track your quantity and quality of sleep.
- Avoid late-night eating. Eating late reduces your body's melatonin and HGH production, which aid in winding down to sleep.
- Clear your mind before you sleep. Make conscious efforts to stop thinking, worrying, or planning. Use techniques like meditation and breathing strategies right before bedtime.

One of the biggest issues that I hear people complain about when it comes to health is that it's too complicated. I've taught health most of my life and...I'm going to agree. Everything is constantly changing to a point that it's confusing. Kris Gunnars of *Healthline* wrote about five simple rules for amazing health and I absolutely agree with him. His five simple rules:

1. Do not put toxic things into your body.
2. Lift things and move around.
3. Sleep like a baby.
4. Avoid excess stress.
5. Nourish your body with real foods.

In sports, I can tell if a player knows what he or she is doing on a given play by looking at their feet. "The feet don't lie." If a player is sure of what they are doing, they have fast feet and move instinctively. If a player doesn't know their plays well, they have slow feet because they are unsure of themselves. When we keep it simple, we can attack it with everything we have. Focus on those five things and you'll be doing pretty darn good!

A Healthy Fairytale for Educators

I would like you to consider a hypothetical story for me. Once upon a time there was a healthy human who badly wanted to become a great educator. This person went to college, studied other great educators, and listened, read, or watched everything the educator could, related to their development.

One day an evil wizard noticed the serious potential that this teacher had to do positive things to enhance thousands of young people and damage his objective to ruin education. The wizard created a debilitating potion that would fool the educator into seeing harmful things as attractive. The ingredients that the wizard chose in his "Fool You" potion were equal parts of:

1. Eye vacumning. This ingredient would provide an ability to look at meaningless objects for hours (TVs, video games, devices) to distract the educator from growing.
2. Food amnesia. This ingredient would allow the educator's mind to forget about using food as fuel.

Instead, it uses taste and availability as attractors to cause weight gain, disease, and lethargic effort.
3. Control illusion, This ingredient would make the educator worry obsessively about problems the educator has no control over. It causes raised heart rate, irritability, high blood pressure, and distraction. This leads to poor performance.
4. Plush comfort. This ingredient provides comfortable chairs and couches within eyesight, drawing the educator in and deterring movement and exercise.
5. Time glasses. This ingredient changes the lens the educator looks through and blinds them from seeing time. This results in weakening relationships, mindlessness, and a sedentary lifestyle.
6. Insomnia. This ingredient reduces the educator's ability to recharge their batteries, keeping them awake until they eventually crash and get a weak recharge.

This "Fool You" potion was a popular one that the wizard had used often and with great effectiveness. The up-and-coming educator drank it like so many others had.

One day, a powerful superhero named "Your Health" appeared out of nowhere to save the day! "Your Health" explained to the educator that the wizard uses illusion and had him under his "Fool You" spell. Sadly, there was no vaccine or quick fix. So, "Your Health" decided to come up with a special vitamin blend that, when taken each day, would diminish the spell's impacts and leave the educator happy and healthy and able to change lives.

The ingredients that went into that pill were equal parts of:

1. Positive attitude
2. Laughter
3. Foods that give energy and life
4. Happy sights, sounds, and smells
5. Quality sleep, rest, and mindfulness
6. Exercise

The educator consciously took this pill each and every day and overcame the wizard's spell. There were days that the educator was tired and worn out but made it a priority. The educator became an amazing Pied Piper to students for a lifetime and they all lived happily ever after. Let's make this fairy tale come true for you and your students.

11

RUN AT THE GIANT

"Fight for the things that you care about, but do it in a way that will lead others to join you."

— Ruth Bader Ginsburg

Do you ever feel like you are fighting a Goliath? As teachers or in our personal lives, it seems like lately our battles are against enormous opponents. We all know the amazing story of David overcoming the odds to defeat Goliath. It remains the greatest underdog story of all time. But what I want to focus on was David's mindset. And I can't think of a better verse to get us into his mindset than this one: "As the Philistine moved closer to attack him, David ran quickly *toward* the battle line to meet him." Boom! He didn't say, "You know, I think I've made up my mind to deal with a problem," or even, "I've decided to fight this one battle." He also didn't tell all of his friends what he was about to do. His mentality was expressed by his actions. When the giant moved to attack him, David floored the gas pedal and actually RAN AT THE GIANT.

Isn't that a lesson for you and me in leadership, teaching, and life? When you are faced with a big decision or a troublesome problem, there are a few steps to the process but eventually it's "Go Time." The question is...how do you go? Do you walk at your giant or do you *run*?

I believe you can go a long way in life on guts and adrenaline. Once you have armed yourself with information to make a decision, how will you execute your plan? I want to be like David and hit my problem between the eyes with everything that I have. David was committed from his first explosive step. There was no chance of turning back once he started running. He brought his own motivation.

The popular motivational trend in education as of late is to focus on your "WHY." And why you do something is tremendously important and maybe the best place to start from, when attempting to begin or rekindle your passion. But once you commit, I'd argue that "HOW" should be your focus word. "How" is your standard. "How" is your commitment. "How" is your intensity for the process. When you decide to act, what does that look like? Are you satisfied with the speed and enthusiasm toward the chosen plan? If I walk at my giant, each step is a choice. There's little momentum in the positive direction. I love what Sun Tzu had to say about this in the legendary book *The Art of War*, "Let your plans be dark and impenetrable as night, and when you move, fall like a thunderbolt."

Sometimes people warn not to burn bridges because you never know when you might need to go there again. But I say burn them, burn them to the ground! If you are trying to make a lifestyle change, a fresh start, or remove something that is hindering you from your goals and gifts….then burn the heck out of those bridges. Eliminate the safety net and the temptation for your mind to go back to status quo. Comfort isn't a word I want to use if I'm making a change. Comfort zones are built for relaxation, not going places. If you want to fully commit to something new, remove the safety net and get moving in a new direction.

Years ago when faced with engineering challenges and problems the Honda Motor Company developed the slogan "Kick out the ladder." I absolutely loved it. It was both a metaphor and a mindset. I believe our human nature is to be passive, non-confrontational and take the path of least resistance. When challenged with problems to solve, sometimes we have to take away our preprogrammed excuses and the temptations that make going back to your safe place easy.

When asked to interpret the slogan, Honda CEO Takeo Fukui spoke of a barn that he found his best ideas in. He said, "Send them upstairs, take the ladder away, and set fire to it. You have to push people to that kind of state, otherwise we cannot create new technologies." That is a brilliant analogy on how to create the mindset for GSD (Getting Stuff Done). He didn't say, "You know, let's get a few committees together, examine statistics for months, take our time, and eventually come up with some solutions." Instead, put them upstairs and kick out the ladder. We will figure out how to get down after we solve the more pressing issue. To me that screams, work with urgency and a focus.

Time wasted is time lost. In your work environment, what mindset does the culture you are involved with have and what would you change? Nothing cooks my grits more than getting to the end of an hour-long meeting and hearing the words, "Let's talk about this more next week." I refuse to believe that in an hour-long meeting a team of professionals either weren't smart enough or led well enough to decide on the best option to a problem. A week later, it will take fifteen minutes for the group to even remember where they were. That says to me that we either have the wrong people or the wrong leader.

Questions to Ask About Your Group

- On a ten-point scale, what is the group's urgency level when tasked with finding solutions? Is this a "kick out the ladder" mentality?
- Are time standards too long, encouraging lethargic effort and procrastination?
- Are time standards too short and unrealistic?
- Is the finished product usually a standard excellence, or is "mediocre" often accepted?
- Is your group composed of like-minded, high-standard, results-oriented individuals or is there an addition-by-subtraction move that needs to be made?

Just Win Today

When it all looks bad, it's very easy to see a daunting problem as a whole. It can absolutely consume you if you let it. The mountain that you are facing wasn't built from just one rock. It was most likely built by a boatload of things and over time. So don't expect to solve all of your problems, or the problems in education in one move. Just as those rocks one by one built the wall, so you shall remove them. But be sure to start with the first stone and start today.

The greatest piece of advice that I ever received in dealing with tough problems was from a mentor, at a moment where I was hit with a serious problem. I knew that I had to hit this problem head on and deal with it in order to move on to better days, but there were going to be some really tough days ahead after I committed to it. Sometimes the right thing and the hard thing are the same, and this was one of those times.

My mentor knew me better than anyone and he said, "Mike, just win today." Those three words of advice were as profound as any novel. You are the CEO of YOU. You have to take control of your mind. Are you going to control your problem or let it control you and see where it ends? Because one of those two things is going to happen.

Years of coaching had taught me that sometimes you will be really behind on the scoreboard. There isn't a magic play to just tie the game. It took time for the other team to get that far ahead, and it will take time to catch up. The only thing I could control was the very next play. If you can somehow win that play, then try to win another play, and then another. Suddenly you look up and you are back in the ballgame. My mentor was right on the money!

So I listened to him. I minimized my view and I didn't look past my today. I focused my mind on everything that the present day had in it, and that was enough for me to handle and do well. So my mindset became, "I'm going to remove one rock from that wall today and if I do that, I'll win today." One day, you look up and you are in a different spot in life. That's how it works. This holds true for most aspects of our lives. In weight loss, it took time to gain it, and it will take time to lose it. In debt, it took time to accumulate it, and it will take time to eliminate it.

In education, I can think of many times when we are staring down what feels to be insurmountable problems. Class sizes, time constraints, standardized testing, and much more. I know that it's overwhelming. Our students feel that way sometimes too. Imagine an AP student who has a rigorous academic schedule, clubs, and extracurricular activities all in the same day, every day. Or the student at the other end of the spectrum who might have made a few mistakes and now is staring at a screen full of never-ending, incomplete assignments. They have walls in front of them too.

In each case, it's enough to make them want to either go crazy or quit trying. That's when you are going to step in and say, "Just win today." By getting our students to focus on winning today's task and moving away their stone, we help them prepare a process that is built for the long haul. If there is ever a mountain in your way, minimize your focus, remove one stone from your pile and just win today.

Choose Wisely

We cannot pick our students, our coworkers, or our administrators but do you know what two things we can pick? Our attitudes and our battles. Both are essential for your health and longevity in teaching.

Nothing and I mean nothing will change your life more than the attitude you choose to have. In any given situation you have an "opportunity" to choose your mind's temperament. I can't understand why anyone would choose to have a toxic attitude, but they do. Everyone knows these people. Maybe they are a narcissist, convinced that it's their world and the rest of us are just messing it up by not following them. Maybe it's chemical or a dysfunction of the brain. And sometimes it's because they were hurt. Hurt people hurt people so they just sadly follow the pattern.

It's a real test of strength and an opportunity for growth when someone fires at you. When we feel attacked the normal conditioned response is to fire back. I saw a reality experiment once where an actor took a film crew and randomly gave strangers the middle finger. It went exactly like you think it would have. Every single person that got that finger gave that finger back. An eye for an eye. They were manipulated like puppets. It was that easy to take a happy person and instantly do damage. Don't you want to be tougher than that? Don't you want to write your own script and to think for yourself? Abraham Maslow said, "If your only tool is a hammer then every problem looks like a nail." So stop swinging it at everything.

In any given situation where you feel attacked, redefine this as an opportunity to get mentally stronger. Anger is an emotion, and it can be managed. Maybe you need to deal with the cause of the anger to limit the effect. It's not really fight or flight. Fighting doesn't always solve it, and running from it is simply procrastination in managing a stressor. Instead of fight or flight, how about we deal with it? Engage the issue in an effort to solve it or make a conscious and permanent decision to release the emotion from the situation forever. Running doesn't cure it, processing your emotions does.

I can remember as a young kid, watching the really old-time reruns of the original *King Kong* movie, which was made in 1933. I vividly recall the gigantic gorilla atop the tallest New York building swatting at airplanes. It was such an imposing image, and I was in complete awe of the creature's massive size. About ten years ago I read that the original gorilla used for that scene was being auctioned and sold for $200,000. It's actual size...22 inches.

How often is that true for you and me? Our perception of ourselves, our problems, and our fears are often exacerbated beyond what is real. You saw your problem as King Kong, but what you couldn't see was that problem was 22 inches high.

Most of us do not like confrontations, but there are times when only a confrontation will do. Day by day, year by year, you avoid your perceived King Kong problem, but in reality, it could have been solved had you just taken the time to engage it and then move on to better days.

There is a story about an old farmer who plowed his field several times a year for most of his life. Lying in the field just poking above the surface was a big rock that caused him headaches. The farmer would try to plow as close to the rock as possible so that he could plant more crops. Many times he would get too close and break his expensive plow blade. This went on for years until the farmer had enough and handed the business over to his son.

The very first time the son plowed that field, he came to the big rock and jumped down from his tractor. Upon close inspection, he came to find out an amazing thing. What appeared to be a giant rock poking through the surface was not that at all. The rock was actually flat on the bottom and didn't penetrate the earth at all. There was no more to the rock then what was visible on the surface. The young farmer easily removed the rock and never had to deal with it again.

Year after year that rock caused the old farmer so much trouble. Had he only taken the time to engage the problem, it would've saved him an amazing amount of time, work, and money. How you look at problems is a sincere skill. Do you freak out when problems occur, or do you see a fixable issue that deserves a rational solution?

Lawyer/Judge Mentality

Did you know that not all motivation is positive? Some of the most impactful and motivational moments in my life have not been positive at all. Sometimes love is blind, and that love is for ourselves. Maybe the best motivation for you and me are things that we don't like to hear and see. Seeing things you despise can inspire because we don't ever want to see that in ourselves. Humility is a dish best served cold. I don't want to hear that I was lazy, wrong, took the easy way out, or handled something poorly. But maybe that was the case. Maybe I need to hear that.

We are guilty of having a lawyer or a judge mentality at times. When we are in the wrong, we are lawyers making convincing arguments for why we did what we did. But when it's someone else, we are judges who are quick to serve up our opinions on others. That's not a winning quality.

We justify our actions so people won't look unfavorably upon us. The first step in changing directions in life is being honest with yourself about who you are at that moment. Calling yourself out can be a powerful vehicle for change. You want to compare yourself? Chances are you'll compare yourself to people you look up to and use the good things that you've done as your benchmarks.

But if you really want to make effective change in yourself…try comparing your worst traits to others that have that trait. It's like looking into the ugly funhouse mirror. You and I don't want to believe the mirror that makes us look ugly or fifty pounds heavier, but that good-looking one that makes us look skinny is easy to believe.

Comparing yourself to the person you don't ever want to be is a strong and powerful vehicle for change. It's fuel and sometimes every bit as powerful a driving force as the positive motivators that we draw from. If you detest the teachers who are doing little, then you can use that as fuel. Harness your anger and use it as your motivation to avoid being like them.

I have a real issue with lazy teachers. The ones who are collecting full paychecks for giving half effort. I get angry because I've seen an amazing teacher who I deeply respect get chemotherapy for her cancer and STILL SHOW UP EVERYDAY to passionately teach kids. I've watched an incredible coach get dialysis and STILL SHOWUP EVERYDAY to coach kids. There are so many teachers, coaches, and administrators fighting through really tough stuff and they are working their butts off for our students anyway. So hearing that a teacher is doing as little as possible with low standards to fight for our students really gets my meter rising.

If a recess monitor is doing the same thing as a teacher, that's a problem. You don't need a college degree to simply be in a room with students. If you could be absent for a few days and nobody would notice...then you are not doing your job right. Not being "that teacher" is a matter of pride in yourself. Those who don't have that usually have an attitude that is not concerned with helping kids or being part of a team. It's simply about cashing a check.

These teachers do serious damage. They let down students who could have been developed academically, emotionally, and psychologically. They let down their coworkers, weakening the team. They let down administrators who are fighting to create or maintain an amazing school culture conducive to a winning environment. If it's true that one bad apple spoils the bunch, why can't an administrator quickly get rid of that apple? Instead, it's a challenge, often taking a long time, even though everyone realizes the damage that is being done daily. As a teacher, I don't want my union protecting them. I want what the administration wants, and that is winning coworkers.

Leaders will often use the phrase "pull your own weight." Do you know where that term comes from? There are two theories, both centered around boats. The first is that it began with rowers in the mid-1800's. Crews would compete in rowing competitions. In an effort to judge each rower's force on the oars, they would compare force generated to their body's weight.

The other theory is that it originated with sailors on large vessels who often had to pull giant, heavy ropes to lift sails and anchors up. They would create many fun songs that are still sung in pubs today as a measure of time while pulling on these ropes. If a sailor was accused of not pulling their strength proportional to their weight, they were beaten or thrown overboard to the sharks. Tell that to a coworker you'd like to see more effort from!

The bottom line is that you were sent into the teaching profession for a reason. It's okay if you have become tired and frustrated. I hope and pray that the wisdom in this book will help to restore your passion and your energy. I hope that the focus you have is on all of the amazing changes that you will make in the lives of our amazing young people.

The world is getting crazier and our kids have a front-row seat via their devices. You and I were blessed to see some normality in the world first, and the volatile times recently. As such, we realize this is not normal. Our students do not have that luxury. You are the best weapon we have to teach normalcy. You are the best weapon we have to teach empathy. You are the best weapon we have to teach compassion. You are the best weapon we have to humanize them when they have been dehumanized. You might be the only weapon we have to tell them that they are loved and have value. I pray for more people like you to join our profession and fight the brave fight that you are vested in. THANK YOU for the battles you fight and the sacrifices that you make. You are our greatest weapon. Keep climbing!

Contact Mike for speaking via his website at mike-franklin.com

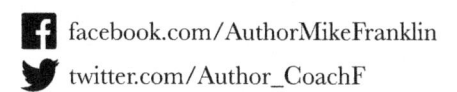

facebook.com/AuthorMikeFranklin
twitter.com/Author_CoachF

Made in the USA
Middletown, DE
20 March 2023